No Brag-Just Fact

THE *SUBTLE* ART OF SELF-MARKETING

Peter K. Young

Street Smart Resources
4726 196th PL NE
Arlington, WA 98223e
www.streetsmartresources.com

Book Layout ©2013 BookDesignTemplates.com

Ordering Information:
Quantity sales: Special discounts are available on quantity purchases by corporations, associations, and others. For details, contact the "Special Sales Department" at the address above.

No Brag-Just Fact/ Peter K. Young. —1st ed.
ISBN: 978-0-692-73161-1

Contents

The Expert 1

Reframing Work 5

The Illusion 9

That Unforgettable Meal 13

Skillsets and Mindsets 17

    1. "No brag, just fact." 19

    2. Know Your Strengths 21

    3. Stop Fretting About Weakness 24

    4: It's Your Differences Not Your Similarities That
Make You Special 27

    5: Your Valuable Failures and Falls 30

    6. On Selling and Sales 32

The Market for Lemons 35

The Awesome Power of a Story 45

The Hero's Journey 49

The Story of Your Journey 59

    Crafting Your Story 60

The Three Whispers 85

The Simple Whisper 89

The Networking Whisper 97

The Sales Whisper 105

Networking Mindsets 115

Concluding Thoughts 121

About the Author 127

CHAPTER 1

The Expert

When I was a boy it was not uncommon on a June afternoon to see me following Slim the Window Washer around town. My mom and dad owned a restaurant in our small town and after I finished my chores, I'd tag along to watch him work. Slim was an artist. He played his squeegee like it was a violin. With a few wizard-like passes the windows emerged from the sudsy water streak free and pristine. And all the while he was so relaxed that his easy effortless work looked like the greatest fun to me.

However mundane it might seem, watching Slim work was my first exposure to an expert plying his craft.

Several years ago I was a member of a creative writing group along with several other would be writers. We'd meet once a week and read each other our latest creation. We were lucky to have a grizzled old chain smoking retired navy chief in our group who possessed a PhD in English literature. Charley could sketch out a scene using a few words, carefully selecting each one to fit the sentence with such care that when it was finished you could smell the cigarette smoke, taste the cheap whiskey and sense the despair that rolled off of the characters at the bar. He'd paid his dues, penning words day after day, millions probably by the time he was done.

Charley was expert at his craft.

I'm a guy who is endlessly fascinated with the "expert" and her "expertise". I'm not talking about those savants who appear on talk shows and pontificate on the current situation (although they may be expert at their trade). I'm speaking of the folks who studied and sweated and practiced their craft until they acquired mastery, that level of mastery which is very hard to describe but you sure know it when you're lucky enough to be one their customers. They may be shy and bumbling in other areas, but Demigods still walk the earth, these sons and daughters of Hephaestus— we name them Chefs and Accountants and Welders and Beauticians and more. All of them artisans, they've spent the time, hours and days as apprentice, then journeyman finally as Master. They've developed and learned the "mysteries" of their particular craft.

From the chef who can take a few mismatched leftovers and serve up a delicious entree to a bricklayer who can lay thousands of bricks each course perfectly level and make it look so easy that even you could do it-- But of course you can't-- it's not as easy as it looks and despite all the how to books and dummies guides, the skill is only mastered after a long apprenticeship.

But here's the weird thing, many of these expert men and women that I've run into along the way, fail miserably when it comes to talking about their work. What's more, however astonishing it seems to those of us who know them, they don't seem to realize how special they and their Work are. That inability to talk about it, to self-market their Work is a real shame.

The truth is that in order to move from Journeyman to the rarefied level of Master, you need ever more challenging work. You need that promotion or that next client's challenging problem to further develop your Work.

To get it, you must be able to promote yourself well enough that others will know that you can be trusted with the responsibility that comes along with opportunity.

Self-marketing gives you a professional edge in the game of life. If you can't do it, you become that guy with one year of experience repeated twenty times. No promotions for you—and forget about all those thousands of dollars you left on the table as well

I'm going to explore the linchpin of the soft skills—the knack of marketing your Work. That's the essence of this book, to help you create your own self-marketing strategy that will accurately reflect your Work yet be subtle enough that you can comfortably talk about it— whether you're a; welder— or a writer— or a butcher, a baker, or a candlestick maker.

I will show you how to merge marketing into your "method of work" so you can show rather than tell your worth.

In order to do that, I'm going to help you learn to harness the awesome power of Story so you can effectively go to market with your Work

---

CHAPTER 2

Reframing Work

When you put your heart and soul into something - whether a work of art, a performance on a stage or sports field, a business, or a job you passionately want to succeed at - then it becomes an extension of yourself. It's not just an object or a game or a business or a job. The end result is not a 'product' or a 'performance' - it's a part of you".

—*Mark McGuiness*

A s I was writing this book, I had a conversation with my business partner about my concept of self-marketing and its relationship to The Work. She understood the need for the self-marketing but she got hung up on the concept of "The Work". Part of it was that her editorial sensibilities were distracted by the fact that I planned to capitalize Work (which was a bit much according to her). Her other issue, though she was too nice to say it, was that I was over the top in assigning so much importance to such a mundane subject.

Most of my blue collar friends would agree. "The Work? Who am I Michelangelo? It's just a job, nothing fancy like you're saying, sometimes it's great and sometimes it's not. I just do it until quitting time and bring that paycheck home to my family." (Their actions overshadow their words. They scoff at the dramatic, but I was taught the meaning of the word "craftsmanship" by a 28 year old welder.)

You might think I'm a bit too dramatic as well, but I'm going to defy my partner's advice and capitalize Work all through this book in order to illustrate how damn important I think it is. Not only does it provide a living for our families, but during the course of our working lives we're going to spend eighty thousand or so hours learning how to do it and then plying it, whether we're employed or self-employed.

Your Work is not — 'just a job'.

My father-in-law told me once that Fridays were his favorite day of the week. He loved the 5:00 PM feeling of quitting time. Then Saturday would come and the euphoria would ebb, damn, it was only one more day and a wakeup till Monday. Sunday was deeply depressing; he found himself filled with dread, for Monday was inexorability on its way.

He'd accepted a promotion from a job he loved, into a new position with a lot more prestige and a hefty raise. The problem was he hated it as soon as he got it. But he was a child of the Depression and in his mind, you did not simply leave a prestigious job merely because you were unhappy. You shut up and soldiered on—you had a family to feed. Unfortunately for him instead of trading up, he'd traded down.

Some jobs are like that. Just like that pair of shoes you bought that looked so classy at first sight, but by day's end they killed your feet.

But they were expensive, so you sucked it up and wore them anyway, hoping they would get stretched out enough that they would be eventually comfortable—but they never seemed to feel right.

I've had jobs that fit me like a glove and some, that no matter what I did, never felt comfortable. I'd ask myself, what the hell was wrong with you? Other people are happy here. Why not you? Shut up and bloom where you're planted for God's sake. Oddly enough it was my fault, not because I somehow failed, but most times because I failed to ask whether or not my choice was congruent with my strengths and preferences.

It wasn't till I figured out that my Work was not same as my job—that the company was a place where I could do my Work. It was a place where I could develop and learn and connect to others in my field.

I began to consider myself self employed, no matter if I worked for a company or ran my own business. I reframed my mindset, took out the word Career and replaced it with a new concept, "My Work".

I began to think of my trade, instead of my job. My trade became a valuable resource— that if I deliberately developed it, broadened it, and marketed it— it would grow into a body of Work that would provide for me and my family no matter what the outside world threw at me.

I encourage you to do the same. The fact is that jobs come and go, as do careers, both of which (as many of us have recently seen) can vanish with whims of a Wall Street banker. In the world there is so much out of our control—our Work is something we own.

> Our Work is the totality of our education, experience and our particular dreams and goals.

It's central to our psychological health. After our children, it's through our Work that we gain access to the self-actualization that is so desirable at the top of Maslow's pyramid. Our Work is the way we are of service to the folks who live around us.

If you were an artist or a composer your life-work gets a fancy label, "oeuvre", those folks take their Work seriously.

You should take your work seriously as well—because the Work defines us.

CHAPTER 3

The Illusion

> *In the long run we shape our lives, and we shape ourselves. The process never ends until we die. And the choices we make are our own responsibility.*
>
> —*Eleanor Roosevelt*

R eframing your mindset toward your Work and away from the career or job has some consequences. It brings with it some new responsibilities. If I was to consider myself self employed, I could no longer ignore the fact that I had to learn to market myself—it came with the territory.

Back in September of 1897, a little girl wrote to the New York Sun asking if there really was a Santa Claus. The editor, Francis Church, answered her in an editorial that assured her saying, "Yes Virginia, there is a Santa Claus".

Sadly, contrary to the paper's response, there is no Santa Claus. There's no Tooth Fairy and no Easter Bunny hopping around either, but many of us still hold on to the fantasy: "The quality of our work will speak for itself."—It doesn't.

It never did, except in the Horatio Alger stories. It's shocking that we don't realize until it's too late that the managers (and customers) in whose hands we've placed our careers, are shown in study after study to be terrible at rating performance.

Marcus Buckingham wrote about the issue in the Harvard Business Review, he called it— Idiosyncratic Rater

Effect, which states that, "as a boss, my rating of you on a quality such as '"potential"' is driven not by who-you-are, but instead by my-own-idiosyncrasies—how I define 'potential,'" how much of it I think I have, how tough a rater I usually am". This effect is resilient; no amount of training seems to lessen it.

And here's the rub — "on average, 61% of my rating of you is a reflection of me".

It's a scandal how much money is left on the table by folks negotiating their salary or entrepreneurs looking for new customers, who are unable to promote the value of their efforts.

It's sad to think of the folks stuck in dead end jobs with faceless corporations when they have the skills and experience to double their pay by freelancing. Problem is they have no clue how to take their skills to the marketplace and leverage them to the fullest advantage to the folks in their network.

Getting ahead, whether you're employed or self employed requires that people notice and appreciate your work.

So the question comes, how can you get me (your customer or boss) to notice and appreciate your work without coming off sounding like a jerk? Even a third grader knows that the self-serving brag gets the opposite of the intended response.

Read on and I will show you the techniques and habits of thought you need to acquire to enable you to take full responsibility for your own personal self marketing. These practices are subtle enough so you'll be able to do them easily and naturally so as not to sound like you're bragging or full of embarrassing puffery.

Self-Marketing is *YOUR* job, don't give away your power— It's your responsibility to nurture and communicate the fruits of your labors in such a way that your work gets the respect it deserves.

A good part of the task of consciousness-raising is to recognize past ways of thought and action. Cast your mind back, can you see times when you let up on your responsibility and traded your power for the promise of security. Maybe you received a lackluster review that didn't recognize your contribution. Maybe you even allowed yourself to believe those less than real opinions and grew to accept your lot.

For now keep those examples in the back of your mind.

Maybe it's time things changed—

CHAPTER 4

That Unforgettable Meal

I honestly promote what I have to offer, consistently and to the limit of my capabilities. I make no apologies for promoting my craft. I am proud of my work, and it is my duty and responsibility to reach people who may benefit from my craft. I can help them no other way.

— *Josh Kaufman, The Craftsman's Creed*

L et's take a little side trip to your town on a warm evening in June. Imagine that you and your friend are knocking around downtown after a movie. The two of you decide you're hungry, so you stop into a little hole-in-the-wall cafe a couple of blocks from the theater. It's a cozy place and the hostess greets you with a friendly smile. She seats the both of you in a private little corner.

Thus begins the best dining experience you ever had. The food is wonderful, the service perfect. And the dessert—oh God the dessert is to die for— a rich and creamy dark chocolate confection that's a whole experience on its own. When the check comes it's a little more expensive than you planned for, but holy cow it's worth it.

What do you think you do in the next days and weeks? You probably never stop talking about the place. You never stop selling the place.

"Boy, what a meal. You should really try it. It was a little expensive, but it was the best meal I've had in years"

I bet you might even mention the place to that random stranger you struck up a conversation with at a cocktail party.

What if you could talk with the same persuasiveness about your work? What if you could do it with no self-consciousness?

Hardly anyone manages to talk about their work with that degree of enthusiasm. And because they can't, they lose out on hundreds thousands of dollars of lifetime earnings. And worse, because they can't express themselves, they don't get a chance to explore their full potential.

Make no mistake, most folks are plenty smart. Most do good work and make a valuable contribution to the organizations or clients they're associated with. They just can't talk about their work; they can't go to market effectively. (You might think that's only for self-employed people, but ask yourself, how do you get that well deserved raise?)

On the other hand, every profession has those impressive few who take their Work so seriously that they leave nothing to chance. They master their trade just like the rest of us. They work hard just like the rest of us. What's different about them? They prepare and market themselves. And they do every bit as deliberately and assiduously as Matt Damon does to assure his next movie role is a good one. That preparation and execution means they reap thousands of dollars of lifetime earnings that the rest of us may let slip away.

Why not you as well?

CHAPTER 5

Skillsets and Mindsets

"....Inside each and every one of us is one true authentic swing... Somethin' we was born with... Somethin' thats ours and ours alone... - Somethin' that can't be taught to ya or learned... Somethin' that got to be remembered... Over time the world can, rob us of that swing... It get buried inside us under all our wouldas and couldas and shouldas... Some folk even forget what their swing was like...

— Bagger Vance

One of my favorite young adult books is "Hatchet" by Gary Paulson. It's a riveting tale about a boy surviving in the Canadian wilderness armed with only a hatchet. It's a journey into to the mindset of the survivor.

We love stories of survival, (especially if we can read them in the warmth of a cozy house while seated in our comfortable recliners). It's fun to dream of erecting a shelter from a few willow branches. We can imagine building a roaring fire to cook the dinner we've just snared. Of course in those imaginings we've had the foresight to pack a handy dandy survival kit the size of a pack of playing cards with enough tools to do brain surgery should the case arise. For our evening repose, we have a high tech space blanket that's guaranteed to keep us warm when the weather dips to 25 below zero. In our mind, we're bravely enduring all this without a word of complaint, without a hint of panic.

In real life if something like that happens, nine times out of ten we're screwed. Nature is not forgiving. We're never prepared. If we're lucky enough to get rescued, the searchers find us cold, wet and miserable; barely alive from the onset of hypothermia. If they don't, we perish.

Chances are pretty good that we'll never find ourselves stranded in the wilderness. We'll never need the skill to start a fire without a match or build a shelter to keep out rain. Even though it's a good idea to have that magical space blanket in our emergency kit in the trunk of our car, we'll probably never use it.

It's odd that we're so enamored with the skills that Paleolithic Man mastered, but so little interested in the skills we need to flourish as Urban Man. If we were stranded in a strange city, say Atlanta, penniless and friendless could we survive? Could we find a job? Build a career?

The skillsets and mindsets that we need to have in order to flourish in our urban environment are the so called soft skills like networking, self-management, and sales ability. They are the behavior skills and anything but soft. I call them the "flourishing skills". The skill of subtle self-marketing is particularly elusive, but I guarantee that with a bit of knowledge and practice you can master it.

But first we need some subtle and not so subtle mindset changes:

---

1. "No brag, just fact."

The old time actor Walter Brennan had a memorable line in the TV series "The Guns of Will Sonnett".

As he was warning one of the bad guys about how good he was with a gun, he said:

"Now my son is an expert with guns and his son is better, "and I'm better than both of 'em -- no brag, just fact.

In my experience, the street-smart way to talk about your Work is to do so in such a way that it is "No brag, just fact". Most people think the way to go about personal marketing is to be like "that guy"— the one who goes on and on about himself and all his accomplishments. Back in my home state of Montana we used to call folks like that "all hat and no cattle". If you've had the misfortune to be around someone like that you know it gets old fast.

In the world of marketing, the brag is called puffery. You've seen an example of puffery at its finest the last time you

> The rule for your story is—no puffery.

looked at a typical high end restaurant's menu. I've no doubt it told of rare gourmet greens handpicked by vestal virgins on the southwest hills of Tuscany. I bet it featured pasta boiled in water melted from ice gathered by the Dali Lama and carted to the restaurant by monks pushing wheelbarrows. And the desert menu, likely written by the chief of Satan's minions, describes sinfully delicious desserts that would make the Pope blush.

The dictionary says that-puffery- is a promotional statement or claim that expresses, subjective rather than objective views, which no "reasonable person" would take literally. Puffery serves to "puff up" an exaggerated image of what is being described and is especially featured in testimonials.

The rule for your story is— no puffery.

Don't say you got an MBA from Stanford if you dropped out just before graduation. Don't invent overblown job titles. Don't exaggerate your success. Don't go into a long winded anecdote about your latest triumph and then try to explain why it was so great (if your listener isn't in the same line of work he won't understand anyway.)

The reason is that hype erodes the essential quiet confidence you need to be believable. Remember you're trying to build trust. Also lies and exaggerations have karma of their own and will catch up with you in the long run— usually at a really bad time.

Worse of all, hype makes you appear pathetic to your listener.

2. Know Your Strengths

"Play to your strengths."
"I haven't got any," said Harry, before he could stop himself.
"Excuse me," growled Moody, "you've got strengths if I say you've got them. Think now. What are you best at?"
— J.K.Rowling, Harry Potter and the Goblet of Fire

You need to keep an inventory of your strengths.

When you ask some folks to talk about their strengths they stumble around the subject and occasionally stutter out some confusing incident or other. After all, most of us are taught to be modest, so much so that it seems awkward to even list our strengths in a calm confident voice.

When the great and powerful Oz handed out the rewards to Dorothy and her gang for offing the Wicked Witch, he awarded brains, courage and a heart. If I had been on her crew and assuming I wouldn't have run away crying, (flying monkeys are scary), I would have chosen Self-Knowledge. It's one of those rare soft-skills that if you can acquire the knack for it, will pay huge dividends. .

The problem is that while our strengths are the things that make us valuable to others, they're often the things we value the least. Familiarity often breeds a sort of contempt.

Bring a person's attention to an obvious strength, for instance, his outstanding ability to deal with uncertainty and he'll shrug it off. "No big deal everybody does that..."

We recognize skills easily; our culture worships skills acquired through hard won effort. But, I think that puts the cart before the horse.

We build our skill base on top of our strengths.

Strengths are your dominant thinking, feeling, and doing patterns that come naturally for you. You grow stronger when you spend time nurturing and feeding your strengths. A weakness drains you and no matter how much you work at it, you don't really improve. It's like going against the grain. Another way to think of this is, for example, when going for a bike ride you need to know what kind of bike you've got, if you take your street-bike off-road, you can make it work, but you're not making the most of it.

Strengths are different than skills. The difference is confusing. When I first sit down with a client to help them build a self-inventory, I usually tell them a story about my friend Leroy.

Leroy has passed on now, but during his life while he was a talented architect, his true calling was as an artist.

He saw the world differently, or I should say he "noticed" the world differently than the rest of us. Whether it was the moon-rise over the gallows frame of the High Ore mine or the seamed face of an old sheepherder, he had the ability to pick up the one or two essential details the rest of us missed. He studied his whole life to acquire the skills to show us what he noticed. That was the essence of his art.

If you were to ask him about his strength, I have no doubt he would have pointed to some arcane (at least to me) technique with pen or brush.

And he'd be wrong. His main strength, the thing that made him unique, was his ability to "notice" differently.

Strengths, as opposed to skills, are personal attributes that you may have been born with or you've cultivated over the course of many years and life experiences.

I like to tell Leroy's story because it illustrates how most folks confuse their strengths with the skills they've acquired. Skills are built on the foundation of the strengths we own.

I want folks to uncover some of their essential and unique strengths and encourage them to build onto them the skills that magnify those strengths, while guiding them away from a fruitless correction of weaknesses.

For example you might have that unique quality of high performance in an atmosphere of uncertainty or stress. Not many people can. Or you might be able to work and deal with the hundreds of tiny details of a project with uncanny accuracy or just the opposite you're fantastic at seeing the big picture amid a mass of extraneous detail. All of those are valuable strengths that you have built your Work on.

How do we do this kind of inventory? For most of us strengths are buried under a hundred forgotten experiences. Maybe it was the fact that you gathered a group of disparate people together to form a productive team. Maybe you were particularly good at analyzing the facts to present a clear picture of a situation. Maybe there's a memory of someone coming up to you and saying, "Damn, Joe you're really good at this."

3. Stop Fretting About Weakness

The effective executive makes strength productive. He knows that one cannot build on weakness. To achieve results, one has to use all of the available strengths – the strengths of associates, the strengths of the superior, and one's own strengths. These strengths are the true opportunities. To make strength productive is the unique purpose of organization. It cannot, of course, overcome the weaknesses with which each of us is abundantly endowed. But it can make them irrelevant. Its task is to use the strength of each man as a building block for joint performance
— Peter Drucker—The Effective Executive

Most people when they want to improve performance think of weaknesses first. Like sixteenth century Calvinists, we've come to believe that any weaknesses are evidence of sin. We dwell on them in that self-talk at 2:00 A.M. when we can't sleep or before we go to job interviews or performance reviews. "If only I could eliminate them, the things that I am really lousy at, I would be a better person, perform better, advance farther etc. etc".

I agree with the quote above from Peter Drucker, the father of modern management theory, that one can only build performance on strength.

Now I'm not a new age positive thinking kind of guy, but I believe it's crucial to a successful life to be well versed with your strengths and comfortable with the fact of your weaknesses.

I say comfortable with those weaknesses, because everybody around you is no doubt eager to "help" you by pointing them out to you. And after a lifetime of being around all these 'helpful' folks a person tends to build an internal story of their life's journey that, well, isn't all that heroic.

Sometimes it's a horrible story.

When we face a challenging situation, we all tell ourselves a story. Every...Single...Time... That's how we deal with novelty. If story you listen too is the horrible scary one, that many of us have lurking inside of us, we are doomed before we start.

You can well imagine Odysseus preparing for his journey then quitting before he started, because the night before he told himself a story about how he was always getting lost as a kid. And who was he anyway to undertake such a perilous journey. And Penelope probably didn't love him anyway. And on and on....

I want you to spend some serious effort on the your story because that negative whisper you hold deep inside needs to be offset with the successes you've had. The perils you've faced and ordeals you've endured and won are a great way to build a whisper to counteract that negative talk. That's the story you need to whisper to yourself the next time you face a challenge.

Some people live in a virtuous spiral. They seem to succeed effortlessly. They are confident. In fact, that's the trait the nonprofessional notices the most--that confidence. So much so that they identify that as a characteristic, a successful person needs to be confident.

The thing is that confidence is a by-product of excellence. Remember your restaurant story? Good sales people are confident for the exact same reason you were willing and eager to "sell" the restaurant where you dined last night.

The goal is to get to a point where you can say to yourself and to others calmly and confidently, "My name is Joe and I'm very good at this. Let me help."

My tip is: Don't try to fight the negative whispers. Merely recognize and identify them and they lose their power. They are not real... just echoes of past emotions.

That is going to be the internal benefit as we build your story. As we craft it and develop it, any negative "self talk" will just be noise in the background. Your confidence will blossom. Your efforts to convince others of your Work's contribution will have a sincere ring of truth.

Sales people who are successful are careful to take jobs with companies who produce great products/services. Their enthusiasm is not feigned. Their confidence is not faked. They genuinely feel they can help you with their product and thus their job is fun and rewarding.

You won't be successful promoting your efforts unless you know deep down to your toes that they have value. If you don't believe in yourself, your goods or your services, why should a potential client believe in them?

4: It's Your Differences Not Your Similarities That Make You Special

Do not underestimate yourself by comparing yourself to others; it's our differences that make us unique and beautiful
— *Robert Tew*

At one time the most popular gambling parlors in Japan were Pachinko Parlors. A pachinko machine is like a vertical pinball machine, but has no flippers and uses a large number of small balls. The player sends balls into the machine, which then bounce down through a dense forest of steel pins. If the balls go into certain locations, they may be captured and sequences of events may be triggered that result in more balls being released. The object of the game is to capture as many balls as possible. These balls can then be exchanged for prizes.

Sound familiar? For most of us it's a pretty good metaphor for our career paths. For example my career life experience is varied and strange. I've been a hard rock miner, a five and dime store manager, a produce salesman, a sales trainer, a trade show producer, a welder/boilermaker, a sales and marketing consultant and a soybean oil commodity risk manager.

My business partner on the other hand has experienced a different career path. Hers has been just as random, but has been driven by a single driving ambition from a very young age— she wanted to be a writer.

She's been a reporter for a newspaper and a legal magazine, a freelance writer contributing to a medical journal, a food writer, pet blogger, an editor and publisher of a magazine and a social media consultant. Along the way she's written a couple of books and some award winning short stories.

Two completely different career paths with one thing in common, they made both of us unique. Our work experience generated a set of skills and attitudes which made our approach to our Work different than any of our respective competitors. I have no doubt the same is true for you; our differences are what make the fruit of our labor special.

Self talk tends to rear its ugly head though; people compare their insides to other people's outsides all the time. Even the most confident secretly wonder that they're just not as smart as the next guy or as creative as that girl in the next desk over. There is a little troll inside that whispers: "you are a fraud".

We think we're the only ones that stood by and allowed vagaries of fate bounce us around in adulthood just like that pachinko ball. We bounced into a job, then a career, then marriage and kids. We beat ourselves up for this despite these are the very experiences that season us and make us valuable.

Unfortunately, we often tend to try desperately to copy others, and then wonder why no one recognizes the unique quality of our contribution.

Zion National and Park and the Grand Canyon are home to some of the most beautifully eroded rock landscapes in the world. A combination of wind and water has shaped and eroded them until they are unrecognizable from the original sediments that were laid down millions of years ago. The elements have worn and tortured them and made them interesting and beautiful.

Aren't there also similar qualities of unique and interesting that make your life experiences valuable? Just as no two snowflakes are identical, no two lives are the same. And believe it or not that's a blessing.

It's your strengths and your experiences that drive the contribution you can make. In order to build on them, to promote them you really need an awareness of their unique value.

The challenge we face is how can we communicate our differences? It's not the similarities that make us special it's the differences, and it's the differences that matter.

How do we show someone who might hire us what we can deliver without going into an incomprehensible long winded BORING recital of our respective resumes?

Why, we tell a story, of course.

5: Your Valuable Failures and Falls

"If you can think
—and not make thoughts your aim;
If you can meet with Triumph and Disaster
— And treat those two impostors just the same;
If you can bear to hear the truth you've spoken
— Twisted by knaves to make a trap for fools,
Or watch the things you gave your life to, broken
— And stoop and build 'em up with worn-out tools"
— Rudyard Kipling

When I was six, I gashed my head pretty good by crashing into a dresser while chasing my brother. It took stitches to close it and I still bear the scar. At thirteen, I crashed my bike and took a spill while showing off for a pretty red headed neighbor girl named Patti. I got a pretty impressive scar on my knee from that little adventure as well. The scars are part of the pains of growing up. Mine are neither better nor worse than any other kid in my town.

As an adult I've gotten scars as well— failure scars. You can't see them but they are there just the same. Like the one I got at 52 from being laid off for the first time. Or the one I bear from a divorce. Or even the one I gave myself from a couple of years of serious alcoholic drinking as a result of the first two misadventures. They were my experiences, certainly no better or worse than the other folks I know. They are unique to me.

I am certain you have them as well.

The triumph and failure that Kipling wrote about, in the opening quote, is not news to us, all of us have faced it at one time or other in our lives. Our failures shape us. Sometimes they destroy us. But they always change us.

Rob Kaplan, when he taught at Harvard, used to encourage his students to pay particular attention to their "Failure Story". Instead of looking back on it with shame and dismay, he taught that facing and valuing the experience reveals the lessons learned by man or woman who emerge from the other side. Mistakes and failure exercises our character.

I find this to be true. In order to really get to know who you are, you need to become familiar (and comfortable) with what you have learned from the failures and disasters you've lived through.

For example, Steve Jobs had to endure the humiliation of being ousted from the company he founded. The humiliation was made worse, whether he would admit it or not, because it was justified. The thing is, Apple's subsequent success would not have been possible without the knowledge and insights that came from his experience at Pixar.

That's the power of failure. If you can get past your shame and knee-jerk self flagellation, the lessons it teaches are gifts of pure gold.

As we move on to creating your story, please allow yourself to tap into the power of your past failures.

If you're lucky, you might even get to the point where you can laugh about them.

6. On Selling and Sales

"You must learn a new way to think before you can master a new way to be." — *Marianne Williamson*

I discovered long ago that the way most folks think about selling is way off base. Beginning sales people tend to see it as a mysterious magical skill that involves lots of semi-mind control techniques used on the hapless customers in order to convince them to buy the product.

Nothing could be further from the truth. My little tale of the night out at the restaurant tells a much more accurate story of what selling is really about.

If you've ever done a bit of business with an expert who is good at selling at the top of her game, the experience is memorable.

She has not swallowed the half truths, clichés and outright wrong ideas that swirl around the process of selling/marketing.

Her world view is different.

Experience has taught her to shift her focus from "what can I get from you" to "what can my product/service do for you?" That simple, but massive mindset change enables her to get over her self-conscious fears and be of service. Our superstar has developed a new way of thinking, learned a few simple skills and adopted some new behavior patterns. She's taught herself an efficient method of communicating

NO BRAG-JUST FACT • 33

with a customer. She's taught herself to interact with people.

She's not necessarily an outgoing extrovert; many that I've met are shy folks. Her sales/marketing approach isn't clichéd aggressive "always be closing" effort you might imagine either.

She's taught herself to be empathic, to listen instead of merely hear. She is not self-involved. She's not listening to you with half an ear while her brain is busy marshaling arguments. She knows she needs to understand you to do her job. So she's taught herself that elusive quality of attentiveness that puts you at ease and allows you to share your issues.

She can tell the product/service's story. She speaks her customer's language to help them understand her product or service and she constantly checks to assure the information balance is as even as possible. She actively solicits objections. And answers them one by one. She then delivers in such a way that they not only satisfy but get referrals as well.

In a fixed mindset students believe their basic abilities, their intelligence, their talents, are just fixed traits. They have a certain amount and that's that, and then their goal becomes to look smart all the time and never look dumb. In a growth mindset students understand that their talents and abilities can be developed through effort, good teaching and persistence. They don't necessarily think everyone's the same or anyone can be Einstein, but they believe everyone can get smarter if they work at it.

— Carol Dweck

Unfortunately, many of us live out our lives without examining just how completely our mindset rules our fate. When we get to be grownups, we tend to accept that our character and behavior is fixed, our immutable nature is formed by some combination of nature or nurture.

While it's certain that many things are out of our control, in this area, we have a choice. We can decide to change, and strike out on a new path, but first we need to be made aware, to have our consciousness raised a bit before we can recognize the possibilities.

You might think that the mind-sets I listed look impossible to master. Put your mind at ease, they are only impossible if you don't try. Just being aware of them goes a long way to learning them.

By the way, this is a good time to start your strength inventory. No one but you will see this so I want you to brag like crazy about your strengths. List them out one after another, and when that inner troll starts to mumble that this one or that one isn't important, tell it to shut the hell up. Keep on writing... Don't let the troll tell your story.

CHAPTER 6

The Market for Lemons

Trust is the glue of life. It's the most essential ingredient in effective communication. It's the foundational principle that holds all relationships.

—*Stephen Covey*

Most of what we know about sales comes from a world of information asymmetry, where for a very long time sellers had more information than buyers. That meant sellers could hoodwink buyers, especially if buyers did not have a lot of choices or a way to talk back.

--*Daniel H. Pink*

N ow, I would bet good money that I haven't mentioned anything so far that you didn't already know (or have experienced).

In the pages to come, I hope to go a long way to convincing you to give up your comfortable habit of self-effacement and have the subtle knack of self-promotion on hand when you need it.

Before we get into all the techniques, let's dig down to the root of the matter and discuss why self-marketing is necessary whether you're the CFO of IBM or the local auto mechanic.

Trust and Information

A couple of months ago I was driving to work and I noticed my engine temperature climbing to the overheating mark.

As much as I hate to admit it, I am a guy who doesn't know anything about cars. So I take it to an auto repair shop.

You probably know exactly how I felt. I was sure of one thing; we were talking big bucks. The mechanic came out, a serious expression on his face and told me that life as I know it will end, unless I give him five hundred dollars to replace my water pump. Oh and by the way, my serpentine belt needs replacing too.

If you've been there, you probably know the questions that raced through my mind. Was he honest? Did he know what he was doing? Was I throwing good money after bad? Was it worth it? Is a serpentine belt a real thing?

My blood pressure climbed to keep pace with my anxiety.

Information Asymmetry and the Market for Lemons

Economists call my situation at the mechanic's shop, "Information Asymmetry". It's the state that exists when one party in a transaction has more information than the other. It's the reason we demand guarantees when we buy stuff. This same asymmetry is also the reason we have a mind boggling body of contract law.

Information Asymmetry is one of those simple, profound, things that we all recognize but until the '70s it hadn't been studied seriously until an economist named George Akerlof got a Noble Prize in part for a paper he wrote about the market for "Lemons" in the automobile industry. ("Lemons" were those cars so afflicted by defects from the get go that they became a constant drain on their owner's bank accounts.) Back in those days, if you were in the market for a car, you had no idea if your choice was the one car out of a hundred that was "lemonized" by being assembled just before quitting time on the Friday before the 4th of July long weekend.

It turned out that just the knowledge that you might get a lemon was enough to drive a lot of people to buy Toyotas and Hondas instead of Chevys and Fords. If you bought a car from General Motors or Ford you expected a big discount before you took the risk of purchasing one.

The greater the imbalance of information, the greater the anxiety lurking in the mind of the customer—Too great an imbalance and the customer either expects a discount or walks away from the transaction.

Back to my mechanic:

- ✓ I had to trust that he wasn't lying about the problem
- ✓ I had to trust that he was competent to diagnose the root cause of the problem
- ✓ I had to trust that he was equipped to fix it.
- ✓ I had to trust that he would fix it in a timely matter.
- ✓ I had to trust that he would charge me a fair price.

That's a whole lot of trusting don't you think?

Information Asymmetry Makes the Customer Feel Powerless.

In any transaction, knowledge is power. And it doesn't feel good to be the one without the power. When it's you on the minus side of the power equation, the only thing you have is trust. (And if it's a stranger on the plus side of the power, nine times out of ten you walk away. But, if you end up buying on the tenth time, chances are you will suffer buyer's remorse if there is any delay in the delivery of the promises made.)

So it's no surprise that your reaction is RESISTANCE. At least until enough trust is established or the imbalance of knowledge is corrected. If the gap is over an item you can feel or touch, like a car or a laptop, you might go to that holy fount of knowledge, the Internet. Of course, if the item is a recognized and trusted brand, that makes things a lot easier. (Contrary to what you may have heard, a brand is not about names or logos or clever bylines. A brand is about reputation, whether folks have learned to trust that particular firm to deliver on the promises its marketing department made.)

If you're the provider, job number one is to correct that information imbalance.

Why Your Last Job Interview was Stressful

Another example might make things clearer. Let's take one that most everybody has experienced— the Job Interview.

Let's take a look inside the head of a typical employer. We'll call her Barbara. She has a problem (a job to fill) and hopes you can help.

But—she's afraid.

She's not sure you can help. She's distrustful because she doesn't know you. And she may not trust her own judgment, which is rational because she's gone with her intuition before and ended up afflicted with "hire'ers" remorse in the past. Hard won experience has taught her that there is a good chance that the information listed on resume is more fluff than substance.

To make matters worse, her own job depends on her getting the right person to fill the slot.

Of course you, the job seeker, don't know all of this. She hides this uncertainty and mistrust. Like all of us, she wears a mask to protect herself.

For example, her masking behavior might be one of the following:

    ✓ Aggressive
    ✓ Quiet
    ✓ Friendly
    ✓ Professional

And if you aren't aware, you might take that mask personally and make some assumptions that aren't true.

For example, given whatever mask she wears, you might think the way to help her get her over her fears is to get her to "like" you.

You should be trying to foster her trust in your fitness for the job instead.

Here we have information asymmetry at its worse. You know you're the right person with all the right skills and experience but she doesn't know that. How could she? The question is what are you going to do to help her see that--You are the right person for the job?

Well, if you were clever enough to be aware of her probable dilemma, you would have known to prepare for it. You would have made every effort to understand where she was coming from and showed up prepared to relieve the information gap. And because you understood her issue and were armed with a plan, you would show up relaxed and confident. That confidence would go a long way to gain her trust.

For example you might have carried in your job references and letters of recommendation. You might have introduced yourself to some of the senior people in the organization and educated yourself on the company's problems or aspirations.

Finally, you would have shown her how you would handle the job. Your task was not to somehow control her mindset— and certainly not to make her "like" you— your job was to understand her concerns and educate her on your specialness.

Trust Starts with Your Bedside Manner

My Doctor is superb at setting his patients at ease. He has a wonderful, calm competence. When he talks to me he gives his complete attention. I'm sure that when I schedule a visit my blood pressure actually drops after my visit.

He's an expert at his work.

Now you might say, "That's the main requirement for a doctor isn't it?" Well sure, but his ability to communicate his expertise isn't common. The office visit isn't about his ego, it's all about me. As he sees a symptom or hears my complaint, he's careful to talk about the symptoms in terms I can understand. He's constantly teaching. He's aware of the information gap between himself and his patient and his patient's anxiety levels and he's careful to eliminate both. He knows that knowledgeable patients are patients that follow directions and in doing so will get better. Knowledgeable patients take care of themselves and tend to stay healthy.

The guy who cleans my carpets is the same way. When he comes to check out the job he is really excited about the work at hand. He hums and tisk tisks. He mutters as he checks out a stain and talks about it as if it were the most interesting problem in the world.

He teaches as well. It's important to him that you understand things well enough to appreciate his work. (And incidentally to understand why his fee is higher than most of his competitor's) In the end you are left wondering if carpets aren't the most interesting thing in the world. As you might imagine my experience with his competition is far different. All they offer is this week's "special" price after a cursory examination and compared to my guy their work is slipshod.

Both of these examples show a great method of working (a bedside manner) that efficiently and effectively begins the process of establishing trust in one's expertise.

If you can't communicate your expertise you might be a scholar in your chosen field but you sure aren't an expert.

Scholars Study, Experts Teach

The first goal of selling/marketing your expertise is to develop the trust factor enough so you can execute the next step of recalibrating the information balance.

Before you can direct your expertise on your customer's problem, you need to develop a method of working that eliminates or at least reduces that information gap, before he will retain you and turn you loose on its solution.

That Method of Working is Called Sales

It's not the same kind of selling you might remember as a kid when you pushed those raffle tickets or Girl Scout cookies—that wasn't selling that was begging.

Selling is the skill set that brings balance to that information gap that has existed ever since man traded a few pieces of flint for some mammoth tusks. It's not some serious magical thing only a few of us are born with; it's just a little understanding, then trust building and educating.

Now that's pretty simple isn't it? No mind control techniques, no bullying the hapless customer to buy, no getting on your knees begging for that job.

Information Asymmetry is so common most folks don't remark on it.

Look back over your past and see if you can come up with some examples of when you lacked the information to come up with a decision to make a purchase.

If the seller noted the imbalance and worked to gain your trust and eliminate the information imbalance—how did the process feel?

Also think back on a time when the seller didn't gain your trust and you walked away. What should he have done differently?

He should have built up the level of trust enough to educate you and reduce the information imbalance.

He could have accomplished that with a story.

CHAPTER 7

The Awesome Power of a Story

Although setbacks of all kinds may discourage us, the grand, old process of storytelling puts us in touch with strengths we may have forgotten, with wisdom that has faded or disappeared, and with hopes that have fallen into darkness.

—Nancy Mellon

This chapter introduces what arguably is one of the most important tools humans have ever developed—The Story.

To be sure fire was important and tool making gave us a leg up but after we invented language, our story telling was the key to passing along the tips and tricks of survival. Today, despite all the digital promises of high-tech communication methods, the plain old fashioned story remains one of our most powerful ways to communicate.

Humans are hooked on stories. Consciously and unconsciously we're wired to make up and tell stories to make some sense of what's happening in our lives. Most of our self talk is a story, which is unfortunate if you don't recognize it, because the negative stories that we tell ourselves are a huge barrier to our success.

This chapter and chapter seven will give you an organized way to think and create the "Story of your Work."

Why you Need a Story

Years ago I had occasion to be thrown together with a guy named Bill on a road trip. I've long forgotten the reason for the trip, but I sure remember Bill.

We had just passed a beautiful farm with one of those gorgeous big Dutch barns you sometimes see in the Pacific Northwest. I was driving and had to swerve to miss a cat which was hunting along the side of the road.

As I breathed a sigh of relief, the near miss prompted Bill to tell me a story about hitting a cat while driving along a winding New England back road.

"I felt awful, "he said. "Here I was driving along on a beautiful spring day, and then I hit the farmer's family cat."

"So I go up to the house to tell them I'd hit their kitty, so they wouldn't be looking for it. Thinking they might want to break it gently to their kids."

"The farmer's wife thanked me for stopping by but it turned out it was not anyone's pet but one of the feral barn cats. I was relieved but it sure did ruin my day."

My first thought was, "Wow, how many people would stop and say something?"

That simple story told me volumes about him and his character. That's the subtle power of a story to impart a vast amount information with a few swift strokes.

A Story is not a Presentation.

A story is sitting quietly in the background while your grandpa, your dad and your uncles joke and swap tales of how things were in the old days.

A presentation is that book report you had to give in the 5th grade in front Mrs. O'Neil's class. Fraught with formality and stilted speech forms, not only is it not fun to give, but it's boring to sit through and nine times out of ten it's ineffective.

If we're going to enlighten and effectively convince folks of the unique value of your work; the first step is a story.

Stories can be parables, novels, plays or even jokes. If told well they can package a concept or a lesson and sell it immediately to a rapt audience. Advertisers use their power all the time--*So should you.*

To do it so it makes sense, we need some structure to build it on. So let's move on and I will introduce you to the Hero's journey.

CHAPTER 8

The Hero's Journey

It is by going into the abyss that we recover the treasures of life. Where you stumble, there lies your treasure.

— *Joseph Campbell*

Humans are masters at crafting a story, indeed for thousands of years the stories told around nightly camp fires were the classrooms for the tribe.

As a result, over the years we've evolved a universal story structure to pass down lessons on surviving and thriving in the dangerous world where we find ourselves. That structure has served hundreds of cultures and thousands of tribes to tell their stories. It's remarkably similar across all cultures. Joseph Campbell calls the structure the Mono-myth or the Hero's Journey.

The reason we're going to use a set structure for your story is that we want to communicate change. Good fiction writers like to talk about conflict in their stories because it's conflict that both changes and exposes their characters. And that change (whether it be growth or decay) is what interests the listener. When something happens to our neighbor we want to see how it changed him. It's the storm and what happened after the waves hit that captures our interest— not the smooth sailing.

If I'm hiring you to do a job of work and I don't know you, I won't trust your competence until I get a feeling of how your life's experience taught you your trade. This holds true for the employer or the client you're trying to impress.

So we build a story using the age old structure provided by the hero's journey. Storytellers use it all the time, so do scriptwriters, playwrights and advertising copywriters. Our structure is a simple one that consists of five distinct beats.

The Hero's Journey in Five Beats

Beat One: The Introduction. (the Ordinary World)
Beat Two: The Inciting Incident. (The Call)
Beat Three: Raising the stakes (The Ordeal)
Beat Four: The Aha Moment (The Realizations)
Beat Five: The Treasures (The Return)

Beat One: The Ordinary World

This is your starting point to tell of how things used to be for you. This shows the part of your life before the tornado (inciting event) picked up your house and swept you to Oz.

It introduces the "old" you and talks a bit about your beginnings.

For example the fact that you grew up on a ten thousand acre ranch in West Texas illustrates things about you that are quite a bit different than if you grew up in a row house in Brooklyn, NY.

This is the time when you had that fantastic job or the boring one. Way back when, before you were tested by life, before circumstance challenged/forced you to re-frame things and move onto a new learning curve.

This part is critical to your story because it will enable you to show the changes your journey wrought. It's the "before" picture that helps to convince others and especially YOU of the valuable gold in the form of experience that you have attained.

Beat Two: The Inciting Incident

Inciting incidents are the random bounces that change your life's direction. One might be turning a corner on a Sunday morning and meeting your future life-mate. Another could be that time you got laid off from a job you loved or the time you got fed up working at that boring job dead end that might have been safe but sure wasn't fulfilling.

Everyone's life contains many inciting incidents, (many times they are disguised as disasters). They are critical to our growth. If you're like me, you probably didn't learn all that much from the good times, but the bad times probably taught you quite a bit. Like Pete Seeger once said, "Education is when you read the small print, experience is when you didn't."

Inciting Incidents are the keystones to our story. In the Hero's Journey, they are the events that pushed the hero from the Ordinary World into the wonder of the Magical World; a world that he would never have entered unless circumstances forced him to. When you think of it they do the same for us. By uncovering the inciting incident, we can show what prompted our journey along a new life/work path.

Beat Three: The Ordeal

The ordeal is the famous learning curve. It's a rare person who enjoys his/her time on that curve. If it's steep, and if the change you must go through is a big one, there can be no doubt that climb is not comfortable. The learning curve of our Work's apprenticeship requires a combination of knowledge and behavior—the knowledge part comes easy but mastering the behavior part is tough. You might recall the movie "Paper Chase", which did a great job of showing the habits of thought and patterns of behavior law students have to acquire. It also did a great job showing how stressful it is to acquire them. Just like the students in that movie, for you in your own journey, everything may have been new and strange. You probably felt powerless because you were not in control. You get to experience your incompetence as well—and that's more than a little tough on the ego.

For some of us there is another harsh obstacle in the process. While the events we call mistakes may end up teaching us the most, we often have to learn from them while working for companies who have little or no tolerance for failure. In that environment, we soon learn to hide from error; unfortunately that denial slows the learning the error can teach us. If we don't learn, we repeat the mistakes. See what I mean when I say the curve is an ordeal?

When I was thirty or so, circumstances forced me to take my first sales job. I remember that time as some of the most unpleasant years in my working life. I was truly awful at selling. I had zero product knowledge and not the foggiest idea of how to go about the sales process. To make matters worse, the company I was working for had a product training program, but no training in any sort of a systematized sales methodology. That ordeal was a major factor piquing my interest in art and science of selling.

I have no doubt your curve was steep as well, I'm sure it was uncomfortable; the important lessons usually are.

"Everyone" knows that nothing good comes without struggle. When we include hints of the struggle in our story it makes us credible.

It's the pressures and the heat and the hammerings of the ordeal that in the end shape us into professionals.

Beat Four: The Aha Moment

At the top of the learning curve, after you've paid your dues, you are rewarded with a series of AHA moments. You suddenly realize you know what you're doing. Few things compare to the feeling we get when we finally begin to "get it".

There is still more to learn, but the process has become easier. Something strange has happened. Something that Stephen Cesi, Susan Barnett and Tomoe Kanaya of Cornell University called the "Multiplier Effect" takes place. We've all experienced this, basically it goes like this: Increasingly as you get better at your Work, you tend to be rewarded, that feels good so, you begin to concentrate on it to learn more about it. Our competence becomes self organizing; we get better because we enjoy spending time trying to get better.

And we're hungry for new challenges, so we accelerate the pace of our improvement.

We've become Journeyman.

If we continue to search out challenges we gradually move to the level of Master. That is if we continue to challenge ourselves, many unfortunates stay in their comfort zones and end up with one year of experience repeated twenty unsatisfying times.

Beat Five: The Treasures

Through his adventure, when Joseph Campbell's' Hero wins, he brings the treasures he's won back to his village. This resolution is the happy ending to the story, Cinderella gets the prince, Little Red Riding Hood marries the woodsman, the Prince awakens Sleeping Beauty with his kiss and wins a bride.

And you've won your struggle to acquire some mastery of your craft. This is the point when your craft truly morphs into your Work. If life-work seems too overblown to you, use the simple word "Work" to describe your contribution. But make no mistake it's become a part of you, inseparable and indivisible, not a job but a craft that you have mastered by dint of hard effort.

Megan Duckett the Accidental Seamstress

Megan Duckett is an Australian woman who won the 2014 Stevie Award for Female Entrepreneur of the Year. She moved to the US by herself as a teenager. She created a business out of the opportunities she uncovered called "Sew What". Her company makes stage-drapes for the set designs of rich and famous. Her customers include names like Lady Gaga and Rod Stewart.

Her story tells of her journey into a successful niche.

Beat One: Her Ordinary World

Megan Duckett started her journey in the design/fabric/show business in far away Perth, Australia. She served an apprenticeship there as a set lighting specialist for rock bands.

Beat Two Her Inciting Incident

She had long dreamed of working in Hollywood, so when she was nineteen she threw caution to the wind, packed her bags and embarked on the 9333 mile journey to Hollywood, California.

Beat Three: Her Ordeal

Like so many others, when Megan arrived, she had to find a job to support herself before she broke into the big time. She went to work as a freelance lighting specialist for a decorating company. It was interesting work with good networking opportunities, but the pay wasn't great by Los Angeles standards. So she made ends meet by doing some minor sewing and alterations for her employer after hours at her kitchen table.

Oh yeah, one more thing, she didn't know how to sew, so she rented a sewing machine and taught herself to sew.

Beat Four: Her Aha Moment

One October while her employer was working a big Halloween event, and Megan volunteered to sew the linings for ten coffins. Everybody raved by how well they turned out and she began to realize that she had a talent for this that most folks didn't have and it could be valuable¬¬—after all not many people know how to sew these days. By this time, she had made a lot of connections within the industry, so she put the word out that she could do sewing work on props and entertainment decor. One thing led to another and a year later Megan landed the gig of fabricating twenty silk chandeliers for The Mirage in Las Vegas.

That's when she realized she was on to something.

Beat Five: Her Lessons Learned

She soon found that she was making more money at her sewing business than her day job, so she quit and opened a business called "Sew What" followed by another called "Rent What" where she rented out props and curtains for the entertainment industry.

Megan's story has all the elements of a dramatic story, and notice that in the telling of it, there's not one hint of puffery.

But, it also falls a bit flat. As I researched it, in the first article I came across, the author neglected to tell of the inciting incident that pushed her out of Australia, so it lacked the drama it might have otherwise had. That article didn't really help us get to know her except on a superficial level. We can see she is bold and certainly adventurous.

The second article shed some more light. Megan wanted to meet Billy Joel and work for him. She traveled 9000 thousand or so miles alone at nineteen to a strange country so she could follow her dream.

It doesn't take much to flavor a story—a sentence or two tells a lot, remember my friend Bill.

CHAPTER 9

The Story of Your Journey

For want of a nail the shoe was lost.
For want of a shoe the horse was lost.
For want of a horse the rider was lost.
For want of a rider the message was lost.
For want of a message the battle was lost.
For want of a battle the kingdom was lost.
And all for the want of a horseshoe nail.—Unknown

Now we're going to use a form of that same structure to build a story of your journey. The old nursery rhyme quoted above is a great example of the unfolding of a story; the cascading events that lead to a conclusion. Life's like that as well. Big effects come from small causes.

"Holy cow!" You might be saying, "I'm a regular person. I don't have much of a story. It's pretty boring, actually. After all I'm sure no hero, so what kind of journey could I possibly have?"

Hold your horses, I say. We're not looking for a Hollywood story; a mighty saga sung by bards of your journey and the thrilling battles you fought.

We're looking for something far more interesting and important to your future. We're looking for the series of

59

events which shaped your mind, your worldview and your Work.

If you're an accountant we want to discover what you've experienced to make you unique among accountants. And I want you to know this well enough, and value it well enough, that you can proudly and confidently explain that certain something that makes your Work unique, and how that 'something' can help me– your client or your potential employer.

Crafting Your Story

The task of crafting your story may seem mind boggling but bear with me— we're going to use the structure of the Hero's Journey to organize things.

We want to develop a compelling story of your own journey. To do that we will build the narrative of you and your Work by assembling your experiences into five interconnected Beats. We're going to make your story logical, simple and easy to tell.

Our goal is to use the age old structure so that you can:

- tell it convincingly to yourself
- showcase the unique aspects of You and your Work

We will start with a question or two about your beginnings then follow up with some "whys and hows" to find out why you made the choices you did and how you got to where you are now.

These are the self-same questions that fiction writers use to explore their imaginary character's lives. Lucky for you, you don't have to imagine it, you lived it.

Your job now is to connect this series of events by questioning "What did I do next.... And Why did I do it.... And how did I feel?"

(Note: Try as best you can to turn off your internal censor. No one will see this except for you. If that inner voice starts to chatter tell it to SHUT UP.)

"I decided to _____ and then this happened..."

---

1. Start with some Key (in retrospect) Decisions

To start the story process, you need to tease out your inciting events. The way to look for them is to remember the major decisions you've made. If you look closely at those decisions, you'll remember that it was some inciting event that made it necessary for you to have to decide a course of action.

For example, at a conference in Portland, I met a woman who had left home as a teenager to tour as an actor with a theater group. They toured all over the US as well as Europe. As you can imagine the decision to join them changed her life.

(Unfortunately, I was not bold enough to ask the question why, or what made you do that? I regret my cowardice, because I still wonder about her story.)

Your experiences might not be so dramatic, but I'm sure you made one or two of those major decisions that shaped a different direction to your life.

Here are a few ideas:

What made you take or leave that first job?

What spurred your interest in your trade?

Who did you meet that changed the course of your work/career?

Take a moment and write down as many of these decisions you can recall. Try as best you can not to censor yourself— just write them down.

2. Now, Pick the One Decision that had the Most Effect on Your Work

If you're employed instead of self employed, I'm not talking about your current job or the company you work for—I'm talking of your Work, your trade, For example you might have been hired by IBM and have title to go along with your job description, say CFO, but your real trade is accountancy.

(One hard lesson all executives learn is that titles are merely labels, however gratifying to the ego when you have them, they stay with the job when you leave. It's a huge mistake to think that you own them— reality is they are only a temporary. Jobs and titles come and go, but your Work is yours to ply for a lifetime.)

3. Beat One: The Ordinary World

This part is made up of a couple of lines describing your life before the decision you describe in step one happened. It could be interesting or mundane. It's a starting point that illustrates how far you've come.

My life back in the ordinary world starts as a newly married guy with a baby on the way. I had a dead end job as a contract copper miner working a stope 5500 feet down in a copper mine in Montana.

Pen a paragraph about yours:

4.Beat Two: The Inciting Incident

The next question for you is WHY? What forced you to make that life changing decision? What forced you onto the learning curve in the first place? Why did you take that job? If it was one of those life changing failures we all face at one time or another, what happened?

Inciting incidents are those circumstances which force you from the "ordinary world" into the realm of the new. Like the adventures you watch on television, many times these incidents are more comfortable to talk about than they are to experience. Folks in 12 Step Programs call them their bottom.

At best, they might be a random meeting with a friend who suggests a job opportunity when you are near to death with boredom and ripe and ready to make a move.

In any case they force us into the process of growth. They make up the drama of our story. And if you have had the pluck to grow in spite of your circumstances, I want to hear of it. It tells me so much about you and your character. We love the story of the hero's travail and subsequent success.

My inciting incident came while working the graveyard shift in the Leonard Mine in Butte, Mt, I dropped a half case of dynamite while stupidly trying to carry it under one arm and climb a man-way (ladder) at the same time. As I watched it fall—lit by the light of my helmet—in seemingly slow motion— and watched the box bounce and split open, scattering sticks all over the floor of the drift. As I clutched the rungs of the man-way shaking with shock, I was astonished to still be alive. (That sounds more dramatic in the telling than in reality, dynamite that is fresh is pretty safe and stable, but even so it sure scared me.)

Inciting Incidents help make you memorable.

Write down a couple of sentences about that incident that led you to make the decision that changed your life (although chances are that at the time you may not have thought so.)

5.Beat Three: The Ordeal

The Learning Curve:

This section describes the time you served during your apprenticeship. Some inciting incident sparked a decision that moved you into a new life adventure and the beginnings of your expertise.

One of the interesting things about the learning curve is how uncomfortable it is. The stages of our learning experiences are filled with "teachable moments", filled with stressful lessons and even more stressful tests. After all when you set out to run a marathon, there is no Easy Button. There are hours of painful, and at times, boring training involved before you acquire the stamina and skills to run such a grueling race.

See if you can come up with an anecdote or two to describe the process to us.

Mistakes and Missteps

This is the time of trial and error. It's important to recall the mistakes and missteps (some tragic and some no doubt comic) you experienced during this phase. Recounting them is an effective way to showcase the skills and attitudes you picked up as a result of lessons learned from by these errors. Because they are mistakes, you can tell this part of the story with a sort of self deprecating modesty that eliminates any hint of bragging or puffery about the new skills learned.

For example, when I share that starting out I was ranked 5 or 6 as the worse sales guy in the entire world, folks think it a bit humorous. When I share a couple more missteps it gives weight to the dues I had to pay. Then in a stroke of incredible luck, I was exposed to the sales philosophy of the guy who designed the sales training for Xerox. It was that one special training seminar that gave me access to the tools I needed at exactly the right time in my development. If I then share that after my "ordeal", I was good enough to introduce and sell products to Starbucks when others tried and failed it gives me creditability without a hint brag. (Remember just the facts...)

Write down a couple of memorable mistakes or failures you experienced and the lessons you learned from them--the more humorous the better.

Your Mentors

Like Luke Skywalker or Harry Potter, you will no doubt have been lucky to find a mentor or two. We all know just how important they are—-having a mentor show up a the right time in your apprenticeship has far reaching consequences for your work. For the purposes of your story, the tales of your mentors add color and weight to your experience, their credentials can add to the image of your expertise.

For example: "I was lucky enough to work for ____. He was real taskmaster. At the time I thought him a real jerk, but he sure taught me a lot."

Mentors come in all shapes and sizes; yours might even be that author whose book you read at exactly the right time in your life that somehow jolted you to a new way of thinking.

Write a few sentences about your Mentor(s), their qualifications and how they helped you get a leg up in your learning curve.

6. Beat Four: Your Aha Moment

Now look back and find a moment or two when you realized you knew what you were doing. That time at the top of the curve, when to your surprise, you had lost the performance anxiety and you were quietly confident of your ability to do the work. In fact you realized that this was the work you were meant to do, you relished the challenge of it.

Write down a short paragraph describing the moment. Where were you? Who were you with? Who were you working for.?

7. Beat Five: Your Treasures

Strengths and Soft skills:

Your journey changed you. Along the way you picked up treasures and gifts. These Strengths and Skills are the things you brought back to your village (customers/employers). They are the things you possess now because of your life's journey.

Take a minute and quickly list your personal strengths and attributes.

Experience

One gains experience in the school of hard knocks, but ironically, it can't be taught. It must be learned. Experience is the street smarts you've acquired on job. It might be job titles you've had or gigs you've worked on.

(Now, I realize that this might seem like that resume you have saved on your hard drive, and in a way the story you're building is similar to one. But there are points of difference, not the least of which is the whole matter of effectiveness. The day has long passed since a resume was an effective marketing tool for job seekers, instead it's become a common resistance response— "Send me your resume and I'll check it out".)

List the dominant strengths, soft skills and work experience you have acquired. The list will be vast and varied, but write it out as informally and haphazard as you will. This is one of those things you're doing for you. No one else will see it, think of it as research for your story.

If you've followed the steps, so far, you now have a pretty good outline to put together a focused tale of how you got from way back there to here.

Just start at the beginning combining what you've written down in each step. Flavor it with the embarrassing, the humorous and the tragic. Then boil it down to a two or three minute story. And practice it.

We're not done yet; your work is much more than mere summation of its parts.

Let's take a look at an example:

Robbi's Story

Recently my business partner, Robbi, unearthed a story she wrote when she was eight or nine years old. It was the first concrete evidence that showed her determination to be a writer even in her early years. Surprisingly sophisticated for a little kid's work, it told a riveting tale of a little girl's adventure wandering lost in the forest. It featured a cast of various and sundry animals she met along the way that gave her advice and helped her to find her way home.

Some years passed. Robbi married, had a baby and worked at a couple of unsatisfying jobs. After a spending a stressful stretch in the jungle of a New York state bureaucracy, she decided to purposefully pursue her dream of being a writer, and applied for work at the local newspaper as a reporter.

The editor told her to take a hike. She had no journalism degree, no credentials she had nothing but the most important thing: Determination.

When I asked her how she finally got the job, she laughed.

"He was exactly like you might picture an old time editor, gruff and profane. I used to bring him a copy of each week's papers with the various and sundry typos circled in red that his degreed reporters had let slip by".

This went on week after week, until one day he was in a bind, and agreed to give her a chance writing obituaries. She soon moved up the ranks and eventually became an editor herself.

Then the newspaper business went to hell.

A combination of changing demographics and the Internet caused the newspapers to sell out or close their doors all across the country. Robbi's paper was no different. It was sold and sold again and finally was shut down.

Next, she did what we all do when faced in a massive upheaval in our industry, she spent a period of time bouncing from job to job, trying to find a situation that fit.

Eventually, her search led her to become a freelance writer. She was soon contributing to a wide range of industry media outlets from legal to food to medical, along the way she wrote a couple of books and some award winning short fiction. But the problem with freelance writing is that given the stresses on print media the work was uncertain at best.

So she embraced the newly emerging Internet, taught herself the software, applications, navigational skills—she learned the language—she reinvented herself as a Social Media Content Consultant.

When we went through the story process, I wasn't surprised that she scoffed at the idea she had anything in the way of an interesting story. People always think the other guy is more interesting than they are.

Again one important reason to create your story is to tease out and remind yourself of the unique qualities that you developed because of it.

How Robbi Built Her Story:

Robbi had several places she could have started her Inciting Incident. The starting point depended on what message she wanted to get across.

Beat One--The Introduction:

She wanted to show how her writer's journey began, so she chose the boring job prior to her newspaper job, but it could have been her daily life at the newspaper prior to the business going to hell.

Beat Two-- The Inciting Incident:

She picked the boredom and sameness of the career as bureaucrat working for New York State. Depending again on her message, she could just as easily have chosen the fact of her newspaper closing forcing her to reinvent herself. It could also be as simple as a random meeting with a friend or even a stranger. Serendipity is a real force in the world.

Beat Three--The Pressures Mount

Once she had the job now what? I'm sure that picking up the skills associated with being a reporter, how to interview, how to quickly write copy that is carefully parsed with all the facts could not have been an easy task. Working in an area where her associates have all the credentials she lacked, must certainly have been a daunting task. Waking up every day with the self perceived need to constantly prove yourself must not have been easy.

Or she could tell of the journey after the newspaper— the difficulty and frustration of leaving the job of her dreams to find another place for herself.

Beat Four-- The Aha Moment

This is the point at the top of your particular learning curve. In Robbi's case it might have that point where she woke up to find herself comfortable in the newspaper environment, maybe after successfully concluding a challenging assignment.

It could also be when she began to realize that she could really help others as a social media expert.

Or as a speaker helping folks with the productivity program she developed called "Conquer the Overwhelm"

Beat Five: The Resolution or Lessons Learned:

This is the "Street Smarts" part of everyone's expertise, the final product that combines learning and experience. When you reach this step you're thinking about how you can help others with your hard won expertise.

In Robbi's case she put her knowledge together and functioned at the top level as an editor of the very paper where she started. She had to use all her skill, her contacts and experience to put out a paper while under the pressure and demands of a daily deadline.

Or she could have chosen that realization that she had become a nationally known expert on content marketing, with blogs and a book written on the subject and in demand to speak on the subject. Once again, the interesting thing about Robbi's story as well as Megan's, told earlier, is that it's a mega-story with all sorts of little stories inside it. It's those little stories that give the process its flexibility depending on how you choose to mix and match them.

Your story can do the same if you put it together as a series of causes and effects, one by one starting with that one (sometimes quirky) inciting incident.

Everyone's life has those serendipitous moments and they are the elements that make your life and work experience unique so the first step is start your outline with the one that seems the most obvious.

Your story is the first step toward the message of your Work, but it's only the first step. Use too much of your story in your marketing and you run the risk of appearing narcissistic and self involved.

For example, it seems like every party I've attended has a person who is enthralled with his own story. His character is the stock "bore" in every movie scene about a cocktail party. You can see him with a wide eyed desperate victim he's lured into a corner, bending her ear with a seemingly never ending story about himself that is fascinating to him alone, but his unfortunate audience, who has no frame of reference with which to relate to the story is soon lost to anything but desperate desire to escape.

Remember the rule is No Brag—Just Fact. In order to pull that off, we need to focus on your customer instead of you.

So that's what we're going to do next—we're going to explore your customer (or your boss) and her dilemma.

CHAPTER 10

The Customer and Her Dilemma

The aim of marketing is to know and understand the customer so well that the product or service fits him and sells itself. Ideally, marketing should result in a customer who is ready to buy. All that should be needed then is to make the product or service available.

— *Peter Drucker, Management, Tasks, Responsibilities, and Practices*

So far we've explored and written your story. Now we're going to move to what needs to be the root of your self-marketing effort, your customer's dilemma.

> **The secret of subtle self-marketing—**
>
> **Talk less about you and your "wonderfulness" and more about your customer.**

Paradoxically, it's when you switch your message toward your customer, her challenging story and how you helped, that you become more believable. As an added bonus, it's a lot more comfortable and natural in the telling as well.

To pull this off successfully, you must look deeper into her life than a mere awareness of her need—in short, you need to know what makes her tick not only so you can do your job but so you can communicate with her (and us as well).

So unless your work involves walking a tightrope across Niagara Falls, you need a customer to bring it alive to me the listener. Otherwise your story is a stumbling account of a series of half-understood job functions.

Annie's Story

I have a friend named Annie who is a beautician. She's spent thousands of hours studying hair styles, cutting and styling techniques. She's put her time in studying makeup and skin. Most folks would consider her expert.

Her problem is that she's not taken the next step toward mastery of her trade. When I asked her about her method of work, her customer and her self-marketing habits, she laughed. "I'm no sales person, I'm just a beautician. I hate that stuff."

(I have to tell you that I hate it when I hear that. Anyone who has spent thousands and thousands of hours studying and mastering something should not be using that phrase "I'm just a _____" to describe their craft and themselves).

Her attitude is not unique, like many others she's chosen the mundane role of the servant rather than the super star who has mastered her trade.

She hasn't come to grips with what can make her valuable to her customer. She doesn't appreciate her own work. Since she doesn't, she can't communicate that valuable information to her customer.

And since she can't communicate it properly her work lacks the impact it deserves---in the customers eyes, perception makes up a good part of the service's reality.

She's not alone. Many folks, experts in their fields, have no grasp of that concept either. Ask them and they start talking about the stuff they've studied or the processes they've mastered. They talk about what they do—-not what they offer.

FAB

There's an old mnemonic that marketers use called FAB, (features, advantages, and benefits). It's a shorthanded way to describe the attributes of a product or service. Features are the physical description, Advantages are the things that are superior to the product's alternatives, and Benefits are the way it helps meet the customer's need.

The Features part is easy to come by—-just look at the product and describe it. The Advantages are a little harder but still pretty simple—-look at the competing product and describe the differences.

But the Benefits, well that's a horse of a different color. To be able to tell how a product helps a customer you have to know quite a bit about the customer, something folks who are centered on their product often neglect to do. It's a serious failing, they spend so much time with their product/service that they become blinded to their customer's reality; after all they're convinced their service is the greatest, the customer should easily see its worth as well.

Susan's Dilemma

Let's consider Annie's client, Susan. Susan is a young professional who puts in a 60 hour week in a law office, in addition to being a full time wife and mother. To say she's busy and her life is stressful is a massive understatement.

Susan walks into the salon yearning for not beauty exactly, but confidence. I've observed that women mostly tend to focus on their flaws. (Seriously— Who needs that side of a lighted makeup mirror that magnifies to the molecular level?)

Maybe she's looking for a makeover or maybe just a haircut, of to get that gray colored out of her hair. She's not vain really. She's a woman putting herself, her self image really, in the hands of an expert to gain a little confidence in a world full of young and slender super models. She wants to be able to relax and say please give me the gifts you've studied so hard to master. She has no problem paying if Annie can make the experience worth it.

It's hard to overestimate the level of trust that a woman must have in order to relax in a beautician's chair. When a women finds someone she "likes" (read trusts), she stays with that person for years. I'm told they even follow them wherever they move. So it's no stretch to understand the degree of trust that Susan has in order to relax.

What she wants and is willing to pay for is an expert who has mastered her trade and has what good doctors have had to learn— a bedside manner. She wants someone she can trust to take her in hand and confidently say in words and actions, let's talk about you and what you need and I'll use my knowledge to educate and deliver it to you.

Unfortunately because Annie doesn't understand that, she hasn't developed her own special way of Working/Marketing/Selling attitude that takes her customer's worldview into account. She doesn't realize that in Susan's case she doesn't just sell styling, she supplies confidence. She doesn't realize the more she sees Susan the better she gets to know Susan's needs. When she builds a knowledge base of Susan's needs it enhances the product/service she delivers. And Susan trusts her more. Annie's practice then jump starts to virtuous circle of service, satisfaction, loyalty. Because she doesn't understand this, her service is ordinary.

Like a good many experts, my friend Annie is too self-involved to think deeply about her customer's needs—that lack of insight hinders her ability to advance her practice to the next level. And the side effect of that often leads her to feeling that she and her service is mundane—that she's just a hairdresser.

Make your Work Meaningful not Mundane

Abraham Maslow, the psychologist, spent quite a bit of time studying human motivation. You might have heard of his Hierarchy of Needs. His work boils down to the fact that we are a bit complex, with a complicated bunch of wants and needs. When the basics like food and shelter are satisfied, we soon reach for higher needs like friendship and love, when one need is satisfied another pops up with the need for actualization at the very top.

Now I'm not a guy who holds much credence with those sales schools of thought that claim the mark of a good sales person or marketer is his ability to manipulate his customer's reactions to his pitch. My experience says that it's far safer to assume that the customer, even though he doesn't know about my product or service, is 9 or 10 times smarter than I am.

I like to remember this because the "method of work" of successful service providers is to first satisfy the basic need then go on to use their imagination to satisfy a higher level need as a matter of course.

In Ken Blanchard's words, "They deliver what's expected—plus one".

This isn't the place to discuss work methods, but my intention is to suggest to you that when you deal with a customer (or an employer) this way, your Work's contribution becomes much more than a mere job of work. You need to be aware of it because you can leverage that into a richer portrayal of its impact on the customer's life when you're talking about your work and yourself.

For example an accountant might say something like--when I do the taxes for my clients I make sure that I've saved them as much money as the code allows and I do it in such a way that they can sleep at night with the sure knowledge that I haven't made a mistake.

> *In the world of service marketing it's the little things that loom large—*

Back to my friend Annie and her customer Susan.
Susan leaves with a new hair cut, or color or whatever. It might be really spectacular but honestly she probably could have received that anywhere.

Annie (if she used her imagination) has several options under her belt to go the extra mile to make her Work standout.

She might for example make Susan feel special by keeping a file in her laptop of each of Susan's previous appointments. With a picture taken after each appointment, she would be able to spend a few minutes talking so she could better understand what worked for

Susan and what didn't. With a file of the beauty products she recommended, she could update based on new health or conditions. Doctor's keep files on their patients, why not Beauty Consultants?

She might send birthday cards. She might blog about new hairstyles and fashions.

Too much? Maybe, but I bet any of those would make Susan feel that she had a real personalized "Beauty Adviser".

My point is if Annie is taking herself and her work seriously, (and why not she spent hours and money to learn it) she should be thinking along these lines and executing some of it, all the while checking to see if her actions resonated with her clients.

The "plus one" Ken Blanchard talked about, when added to her working methods could add up to "raving clients" instead of merely satisfied ones. That adds up to thousands of dollars not to mention huge gains in job satisfaction.

Then Annie should carefully build a story about her Work that shows how she transforms her customers feelings about themselves and enables them to be more confident and successfully.

Her work story then becomes part and parcel of her service's contribution.

(I guarantee her perception about her work would change for the better. Never again would she refer to herself as just a beautician!)

The Before and After State

Given all the above, we're going to move to the next stage of our marketing.

How can we tell our customer's story in a way that showcases our Work?

Remember, the rule is always "no brag...just fact". As I mentioned, the important part of our tale is how the customer's life was changed because of us.

Customers (and employers) deal with us for three basic reasons

- ✓ Because they can get something they didn't have before.
- ✓ Because they can feel something they didn't feel before.
- ✓ Because they get rid of a problem that troubled them.

Our message needs to key in on the customer's transformation. We want to look at her before and after state. What her life was like before she took delivery of whatever you provided and what her life was like afterwards. Results both physical and emotional are what folks readily understand (and appreciate).

So if you're a neurosurgeon don't go on and on about the procedures you use to repair the human spine.

Instead tell a story—

"We had a patient a couple of years ago, who fell off a ladder and was facing a lifetime of pain at best or paralysis at worst. We went in and after 9 hours of surgery repaired the damage enough so it could heal. Guy teaches modern dance and performs in the annual Nutcracker at Christmas..."

Your job now is to pick a customer and learn her story. Delve a little deeper, go beyond the simple fact of your work and imagine the emotions she might feel after you've delivered your services. Better yet, pick out one of your ideal customers and see if you can tease out more details on their experience with you.

Okay we've got your story and now we've defined your work your contribution to folks you serve. Next we're going to talk about some actual methods of self marketing you can adopt today in order promote your work without a hint of puffery.

CHAPTER 11

The Three Whispers

Listen to me, the loudest one in the room is the weakest one in the room.

— Frank Lucas, "American Gangster"

Most everyone these days is familiar with the Elevator Pitch. The phrase is credited to Ilene Rosenzweig after hearing of her then boyfriend Michael Caruso's efforts to pitch story ideas to fast moving Tina Brown, the editor in chief of Vanity Fair, sometimes literally during the space of an elevator ride.

I suspect it's been around a lot longer than that. The idea is simple. An entrepreneur who wants to pitch a product to a prospective investor should be prepared to do so with admirable brevity within the space of an elevator ride. (They're busy people after all and it needs to be "just the facts, Ma'am. Just the facts—").

The concept caught the popular imagination and today you can find hundreds of articles on the Internet on how to pull off an effective elevator pitch.

There's a problem however, most of us are not journalists, and the elevator metaphor is not really adequate to the task of introducing our Work. We're interested in effectiveness not just brevity. We want to be memorable as well, so we need a bit more romance than just the facts ma'am.

Another problem is that the elevator pitch is—well, it's a little too "pitchy". Every time I hear the word pitch, I picture myself walking down a carnival boardwalk with the guys in the booths (pitchmen) on both sides clamoring for my attention, (and like you, I'm staring straight ahead careful not to catch their eye).

For most of us pitching feels uncomfortable, undignified and, if we're honest, a bit desperate—-we especially have a tough time doing so to a stranger.

So if we don't pitch—-what then? We know we need something. Anyone who is street-smart knows that one should be prepared at all times and at all places to talk about one's Work because opportunity is serendipitous, it knocks when you least expect it. It's common sense to have that 'something' prepared.

I'm going to suggest that instead of pitching—-you whisper.

The Expert Whispers

I like the thought of a story that whispers your mastery of your craft. A story carried in your personal marketing toolbox—-one that's interesting enough to hold someone's attention but contains not the slightest hint of a brag or self promotion.

It should be conversational, free of jargon. Its goal is to communicate a bit more of your work. It should also spur the response--"That's interesting how do you do that?"

So instead of creating a Pitch, we're going to build some Whispers.

We're going to delve a bit into your history (your story), talk a bit about your work's path, talk a bit about your choice of customers to serve and then wrap it up with the advantage that this has given you over your competition.

In addition, we're going to focus on the effect your work has, rather than your work's methodology.

And we're going to do it in a way that "shows rather than tells" so we can minimize any hint of puffery or self promotion. The whispers we create won't be pitches and they won't be presentations—-they're going to be stories.

The Three Whispers

We're going to create and practice not one but three whispers of differing lengths, because just like my little blond friend Goldilocks after some real world testing at the Bear's house, we want the story that's just right for the situation. And if you're like most folks you need three.

So we're going to develop three stories, each of which builds on the former, each in turn takes a little more time to present, but gives an increasingly richer picture of your Work.

CHAPTER 12

The Simple Whisper

> *Three stone masons in the Middle Ages were hard at work when a visitor came along and asked them what they were doing.*
>
> *The first stone mason was hard at work, sweat beading his brow. "I am cutting this stone," he grumbled.*
>
> *The second stone mason, though less distraught, responded with a deep sigh, "I'm building a parapet."*
>
> *The third stone mason replied with a radiant face, "I am building a beautiful cathedral that will glorify God for centuries to come."*
>
> — *Author unknown*

Several years ago I found myself at a convention cocktail party. You know the kind, nice setting, surrounded by folks you barely know, everybody milling around starting up casual conversations. Someone came up to me—(as I was standing in a corner trying to figure out how soon I could escape).

"So", he said, "What do you do?"

I answered, as most of us do, with some general comments, starting and stopping, reaching for words to describe the essence of my work to someone who doesn't live in the same world as I do and has no hope of understanding it.

As I sat in my room afterwards, I wondered why it was so difficult to explain my Work. I'm a professional sales person. I've made hundreds and hundreds of presentations over the years, talked to CEOs about fairly complex subjects and sold millions of dollars worth of ideas and products. I love my Work, why the hell was it so difficult and frankly uncomfortable to explain it.

When my business partner and I discussed this, I was a bit surprised to find she had the same struggle trying to answer the same question.

I asked her to explain.

"I have a terrible time answering that question. When I tell them, I'm a blogger; they assume it's a hobby.

If I mention content creation, they look at me with a look that clearly says they haven't the slightest clue of what that means, let alone why it's so important.

When I say I'm a writer they assume I'm one of those unfortunates starving in a garret, shivering with the cold, maybe wearing fingerless gloves while I pen my first novel."

"Just like you", she said. "I always struggle with it and I have no idea why."

The Simple Whisper

The answer to this situation was simple; we both had neglected to prepare ourselves for the question.

We're going to remedy this common problem. Starting with this chapter we're going to craft three whispers.

The first of these is the "Simple Whisper". It's a quick answer to the casual question, "What do you do for a living".

Your Simple Whisper is essentially a quick clear brand statement—it's not a job label like Butcher or Baker or Candlestick Maker—it's not a fancy schmancy mission statement and it's definitely not puffery. Instead it's a simple little tale of your work's effect. Its purpose is to separate you from the rest of the folks in your field in your listeners mind. If you tell it right it makes you memorable. It's easy to deliver because it's light and fun.

If you practice it (and you should) and deliver it with confidence, it's a quick and effective form of self-marketing— one that everyone should have in their toolbox.

In short it's a way for you to speak for your Work. Remember, if you don't no one else will.

Many people stumble because they try to make a complex answer the simple question, "what do you do?" They try to make someone understand by talking about the tools and methods they use in their work or try to describe a typical day and the problems they face. Because their listener usually has no frame of reference to understand, it soon becomes just so much noise, once heard it's quickly forgotten.

To make matters worse, unless you're pretty thick skinned and unaware, as you see your listener's eyes start to wander, you either try harder, or end up letting your explanation trail off. Either way you walk away from the conversation vaguely embarrassed.

The fact is that unless you do the same thing as I do for a living, it's like trying to explain color to a blind person. It becomes easier to just attach a company name like I work for Microsoft or work label like I'm an accountant, and walk away. That's why it's no surprise that you often see folks at an event sticking with others in their profession or company instead of going out and meeting new people.

For example, I worked for a number of years as a journeyman boilermaker. Now, most people have no idea what a boilermaker does. Who uses big boilers anymore? I could go on and on about the jobs we worked on, the weld types or the different wire and rod we used, or whether we used TIG or MIG welding. I could even speak to the difficulty of learning to run a bead of weld, when one's body is contorted into a small space, a clean bead that needs stand up to rigorous X-ray testing. As interesting as that is to me, you would soon be fast asleep at such descriptions.

But if I told you about building the massive wind towers that generate megawatts of electricity in eastern Washington. Towers that are so heavy that their weight defies ordinary description—-you might get an immediate picture of the results of our labor. You might even ask some follow-up questions.

Your Simple Whisper is the practiced reply to the question, "What do you do?" It's the first of the whispers and the one you will use the most. So take some pains to construct it. We want it to be simple, short and memorable. We want it to engender the response, "That's interesting, how do you do that." It shouldn't be difficult to do, as long as you have done your homework on your story and delved into your customer's dilemma.

Crafting your Simple Whisper

Your Simple Whisper is made up of three or four sentences:

1.   *Your name (if you haven't introduced yourself), and a POSITIVE description of your working attitude*

When I meet someone who has positive upbeat attitude about what she does, I'm automatically a bit more interested in her. A positive statement tells quite a bit about how in control she is of her destiny. It's a power statement. It shows that they have done the work to make themselves satisfied with their life. Note that I'm talking about her "Work" not her employer's. Even if she hates her employer, she needs to show she loves her work.

If you're lucky enough to have an unusual name, accentuate it with a comment about its spelling or origin. I have a friend whose name is Straatviet and he always jokes that even the guys who worked at Ellis Island couldn't misspell it as much as his friends do. (and after you meet him you sure remember his name.)

2. *A simple sentence of describing your customer's dilemma*

This is the heart of it. This is the most important part of it. Offer a quick picture of your customer's dilemma. Remember we want to talk about your Work's effect. To do this we check out a typical customer's "life before they met us" and construct a sentence that highlights her issue(s).

Note that I'm using customer in a broad sense; our customer could refer to a person, company or community.

3. *A sentence describing how you resolved the dilemma*

Finally we want to show her "after" state, her satisfaction with the problems resolution. How her life was made easier. We want to invite the question, "That interesting, how do you do that?"

Resist the temptation to go into your works methodology unless you can state it so simply that a fourth grader could understand it. And be careful with jargon, even though the temptation is there to use it to show you're knowledgeable.

It sounds simple and it is, but that doesn't mean it's easy to create one that's memorable.

For example, if I were building one I might say:

Hi my name is Pete Young. After years of being in sales and training sales people, my latest project is a rewarding one.

I work with folks who are masters of their craft but who have a difficulty talking about it and marketing it.

I teach them the three expert whispers and help them learn to market themselves effectively.

Here's Robbi's Simple Whisper.

My name is Robbi Hess and I have my dream job.

I've been a professional writer for 20 years and for the last 6 years or so I've had the pleasure of working with companies in the pet industry who have great products but are lost when comes to online marketing.

I write good effective content that helps them to create an atmosphere on their website that builds a sense of community for their customers while showcasing their products

CHAPTER 13

The Networking Whisper

Someone you haven't even met yet is wondering what it'd be like to know someone like you

—Ian Thomas

When your new found friend at a business meeting hears your Simple Whisper and asks, "Wow that's interesting, how do you do that?" — that's your cue to trot out your polished and practiced Networking Whisper.

Networking groups have sprung up in cities all of over the world. These are gatherings where folks stand up introduce themselves and talk about their Work. In days gone by, the same sort of thing took place on Sunday afternoons in church basements over coffee and cookies after Sunday services or at Kiwanis meetings on the first Tuesday of every month.

When you have to stand up and introduce yourself at one of these meetings—-you need to be armed with your polished and practiced Networking Whisper.

This second whisper is a bit more involved. This one weaves more of your customer's dilemma into the story. It frames and showcases your Work by showing what you do for your customer. You're going to tell of your Work's effect on the customer's life. And because you use a story to tell it, you can be comfortable even confident in the telling.

Crafting Your Networking Whisper

In order to build your Networking Whisper start with your simple Whisper then add a bit more about your customer:

1. *Using simple terms (no jargon) construct a one or two sentence story about your customer's life before he interacted with you.*

You're going to show the nature of his situation:
- ✓ What did your customer NEED in the "Before" state?
- ✓ How did your customer FEEL in the "Before" state?
- ✓ What was your customer's STATUS in the "Before" state?

When someone asks what you do for a living, instead of a long explanation of your work, you're going to turn the conversation away from you and introduce your customer and her situation.

For Example:

"One of the most trying times in a person's life is when they've had their house burn down. A couple of months ago, I had a client whose house burned down on Easter Sunday as the family was at church (This shows the event that created the need.)

As you can imagine they were in a serious state of shock (This points out how the customer felt before.)

The thing is that folks like them are at disadvantage dealing with their insurance company about their claims. It's an incredibly complicated process" (This explains how the customer felt inadequate to deal with the situation.)

Now that's a pretty good description of the before state.

2. *Now we follow up with another one or two sentence description of our customer's life AFTER dealing with us. Just the facts with no brag.*

Here's step two from our insurance consultant:

"...For example while you can list some of the obvious valuables in your home, I bet you're like most folks and have an incredible amount of money tied up in mundane things that don't come to mind immediately, like bath towels and bedding. These things are often overlooked and cost a fortune to replace. My service provides a "go between" to help them negotiate their claim with their insurance company that ultimately saves them numerous headaches and thousands of dollars."

(I bet you'd remember that guy. I bet you'd ask for his card—-to have just in case.)

The thing to key in on is the customer's transformation. We want to look for the before and after state. That's what folks readily understand and identify with.

Remember our friend the neurosurgeon? If he wanted people to understand his contribution, he shouldn't go on and on about the procedures he used to repair the human spine--—instead he should tell his patient's story.

Example:

"We had a patient a couple of years ago, who fell off a ladder and was facing a lifetime of pain at best or paralysis at worst. We went in and after 9 hours of surgery repaired the damage enough so it could heal. Guy teaches modern dance and performs the in the annual Nutcracker at Christmas."

Robbi's Networking Whisper... "That's interesting how do you do that?"

As you might remember from her story, Robbi is an experienced writer with a journalism background. She has found a niche as a Social Media Consultant specializing in content creation.

Here is how she went about building her Networking Whisper:

1. *Exploring Customer Molly's Dilemma-- "Her Before State"*

"I met Molly at Super Zoo a couple of years ago. Super Zoo is a big show for pet retailers in Las Vegas. We ran into each other as we sipped some coffee and rested our feet.

Molly and her husband manufactured a line of natural organic dog treats. Her husband, who was a veterinarian, had gotten frustrated at the really poor quality and downright unhealthy products on the market, so along with Sharon who is a food technologist they started baking them in her kitchen.

Neither one of them was tech savvy, so like most businesses, who know they need to have a presence on the Internet, they hired a company to build them a web site.

The company built it and Molly had had a photographer friend of mine take some pictures of our product, which turned out really great. The web designer put them up along with a price list.

Neither one of them had time to do anything with it, so they hired a friend who fancied herself a writer to post some blogs and do some facebook posts. But the site just sat there, a reminder of an expensive mistake...I guess she was resigned and more than a bit cynical about the whole online thing. Really disappointed as well, they had been counting on that to bring their growth to the next level."

2. *The Answer to Robbi's Customer Molly's Dilemma "Her After State"*

"People especially merchants tend to think of marketing on the web like they do about advertising. You know, like a

newspaper ad or a radio spot. It's a static strategy that is guaranteed to fail because there is just too much noise on-line. And suspicion as well, spam is so endemic that most folks ignore or distrust anything they don't know. It doesn't help that consultants tend to throw jargon around to impress which instead ends up confusing the client. It doesn't help that web-marketing is so often over-promised and under-delivered.

I told her my first job was to give her a mini education on strategy and expectations so she could use her experience and expertise to guide me on the next step which was to build a community with her customers, a close knit tribe that would do a lot of her advertising by word of mouth.

We talked about the way I would go about to start to reach out to that community is through superior content that speaks to the everyday events and challengers they and their pets face. Like health and exercise or articles dealing with traveling with their dog."

Okay, using this information, Robbi had more than enough to come up with her Networking Whisper:

Robbi's Networking Whisper

"The easiest way to explain what I do is tell you about one of my long time customers, Molly. She and her husband own a pet snack company. When I met her she was really frustrated and cynical about the promise of marketing on-line. She had a pretty good website built for her company by an expensive designer that was not generating anywhere near enough sales considering on how really cool her product line was. She had

hired a friend who fancied herself a writer to write the page copy and some blogs, and was freaked because the writing was terrible and she was going to have to fire her friend.

My first job was to give her a mini education on web strategy so she could use her experience and expertise to guide me on the next step which was to build a community out of her customer base. We built a close knit tribe that did a lot of her advertising by really powerful word of mouth.

We developed an ongoing editorial calendar so we could reach out to that community and provide superior content that speaks to the everyday events and challenges they and their pets face; like health and exercise or articles dealing with traveling with their dog."

Her business is up by 25% and still growing.

CHAPTER 14

The Sales Whisper

The purpose of a pitch isn't necessarily to move others immediately to adopt your idea. The purpose is to offer something so compelling that it begins a conversation, brings the other person in as a participant, and eventually arrives at an outcome that appeals to both of you.

—Daniel Pink, To Sell Is Human: The Surprising truth About Moving Others

I magine yourself in the following situations:

--You're sitting down to a meeting with a new client. He doesn't know you and you need to know more about his situation. How do you start the meeting? Do you do what the sales pros do and have your own methodical way of going about the "new customer interview"? Or do you ramble and mumble with some random small talk in a desperate attempt to find a way to segue into business.

--You find yourself in front of a woman who could be your next boss, but first you have to get through the dreaded job interview. Do you have a prepared and practiced way to answer the question? Something like: "So tell me a little about yourself?" Can you tell a story about yourself that begins the process of showing her you can do the job?

How the Pros Do It

The sales craftsmen I've known over the years have a structured methodical way of going about their work that is key to their competence. Mad, glad or sad they cover all the bases meticulously. They take pains to assure excellence. If you ever have the opportunity to observe a gifted sales person, you will notice they have a definite way of conducting a call.

They always start by introducing themselves and their company. They have learned not to assume you know anything about them or their product. They know assumptions cause friction in the smooth process of communication—-you should do the same and be as well prepared as they are.

That's what the Sales Whisper will do. Please don't be intimidated by the name, it's a bit more complicated, it's a bit more lengthy, but it's still a story. We build it atop your previous whispers with a carefully leavened pinch or two added to your Work's story.

Let's look at what we want it to accomplish:

- ✓ We want to begin to establish trust.
- ✓ We want to (subtly) build credibility as an expert in our craft. (Credibility and Trust building are the overriding goal of all of the whispers.)
- ✓ We want to begin to establish a working relationship. Note: we're not looking to be friends (although we may end up that way).
- ✓ We want be able make a comfortable segue into a conversation about the prospective client's need.
- ✓ Finally, we want it to be pressure free both for ourselves and for our listener.

In order to do *all of those things, we tell a story.*

The Sales Whisper

1. Find Your Inciting Incident:
One reason I asked you to write down your "hero's journey" was to uncover your inciting incident; the one thing that happened to you to set you on your Work's path. It doesn't have to be dramatic, it could be something simple like— "I've always been fascinated by _____."

Whatever you choose, your inciting incident makes you memorable and nicely sets up the beginning of this "Whisper". It makes you credible because it gives the reason you spent the time developing your craft. Remember we want to show not tell.

For example:
"When I was 12 years old my Uncle Jim went bankrupt. It destroyed his life. It frankly had a huge effect on me as well and set me on a path to help other folks handle their money...."

"I was laid off in my twenties with a wife and two little kids to feed. The only job I could find given my level of experience was a sales job. The problem was that I really sucked at selling, so I set out on a journey to learn, figuring if others could do so could I...."

2. Your Apprenticeship:
You've got your inciting incident; the next question is how did you respond to it? What did you do next? Now you tell about the stages of your journey to master your Work. Maybe you mention the mentors who taught you. Maybe you mention the struggles. People know that worthwhile things aren't free of effort and time. That particularly holds true for one's "apprenticeship". Everybody knows that great talents sweat blood to attain that talent, so give them a bit of a story about your journey. Obviously you can take your tale of suffering too far, but do add a bit of drama.

For example:

"I've always wanted to be a writer, but the thing is writing good copy has to be learned. People can teach you grammar, but have to put in the time writing, hours of it, some say 10 million words in order to achieve any level of mastery. In my twenties, I talked my way into a news room first as a reporter later as a managing editor. When the newspaper business started to tank, I freelanced for a while, but soon found a home in the fascinating world of social media marketing. It was a match made in heaven for me and I've been helping companies build a community with their customers for 15 years now."

3. Your Specialty:

Your specialty is the marriage between your strengths, your training and the market. It's the job you do best. Specialization helps define expertise.

A million or so years ago, when a really smart cheetah got tired of being hungry and watching the lions get the lion's share of the wildebeests she switched her prey of choice to antelope figuring her speed would give her an edge. She developed a specialized hunting technique.

That guy who claims to be master of all trades is rightly assumed to be master of none. When I have a problem I want a guy who is an expert in knowing the solution to it.

4. Your Niche:

Few things can whisper more about your expertise than the customers you serve.

Your niche is the field where you ply your craft; it's where your customers live. It's a place where the inhabitants have their own special language when they talk about their customers and their challenges.

Your knowledge of your customer's language and common challenges is the real key to the marketing of your expertise. If I'm your prospective customer, when you talk to me in my language and have a pretty good working knowledge of what's it's like for me to compete in my market, it doesn't take but a few quick sentences to show me that you know what you're talking about.

For example:

"I specialize in helping natural food companies place new items in the market. Today the grocery store shelves are so crowded that most new products fail not because they are not good but because there has to be a well thought out strategy behind their launch. You either have to be smart or have a huge bank roll to launch new items. You have to be careful when you choose the distributors you work with".

5. Your USP and your competition:

Your USP (unique selling proposition) is the "story" about what sets you apart from your competition. We've explored how your history has formed this uniqueness.

Now we're going to talk about the way your Method of Working gives this uniqueness value. It's about how you deliver the benefits of your Work.

Speaking of your competitors, here is another important rule—-share the positives about your work instead of waxing negative about your competition.

Concentrate on your benefits and you then essentially infer that your competition's work is commonplace next yours.

Robbi's Sales Whisper

Here's how Robbi took some key points from her story and built her Sales Whisper to use when she has a meeting with a new client.

Remember Molly? She is the customer who along with her husband ran a pet snack company. Robbi's sitting down with her for their first meeting. It's her version of the new client interview. Her carefully built sales whisper is the first part of this interview.

Introduction:

Hi my name is Robbi Hess. Before we get started let me tell you a bit about myself and the way I work.

I've been a professional writer for 23 years. I think I've always wanted to be a writer and in my late twenties I managed to talk myself into a job at my local newspaper as a reporter.

Inciting Incident:

It was a great career first as reporter and then later as a senior editor, but as the Internet started to slowly kill the newspaper business I was forced to make a switch.

When a friend of mine invited me to consult on the content for her new web site, I agreed to write some content for her home page.

Apprenticeship:

I thought it would be easy, I was a pro after all; in my career I've written millions of words, but I was soon disavowed of that notion. Creating good content for online marketing is a tricky blend of art and science. You're trying constantly to build and maintain a community of loyal customers. Good content that is social and unselfish enough to build followers yet mercantile enough to sell product is a skill I had to acquire, because even in those early years there was so much noise. All that added up to a really steep learning curve made worse because it was all new.

Specialty:

Because of my experience I have a knack for writing good effective content. I don't take on the technical stuff site building or design, but I do have familiarity with quite a bit of the software. My job is helping my clients first build their business story, and then together we collaborate to build a community of customers. The goal is to do it well enough to be heard over all the noise online.

Niche:

While I do have a few clients outside of it, my niche is the pet industry. Pet owners tend to have a passionate relationship with the companies they do business with. I understand them and have a good feel for their hot buttons. My customers are manufacturers with sales in the 5 to 10 million dollar range.

Her USP:

This business is full of overblown promises and under delivered results. That fact has shaped the way I work with a client especially a new one. I've found that I can't succeed without a close collaboration with the client. So I start off with a detailed marketing analysis. Social media is only a part, an important part to be sure, but a part that needs to mesh and accentuate the businesses' marketing effort as a whole. Next, I move to the interview stage where we fully develop some simple goals, plans and expectations. After that, comes the review stage, we meet every three months so we can track our progress.

My claim to fame is based in part that I write fast, but it's my ability to tease out the salient facts about the product and its emotional relationship to the customer, that makes all the difference. I've found that my client's already know the important stuff they just need some help bringing it to the fore.

Let's look at our requirements:
- ✓ Did she make a start at balancing the information gap?
- ✓ Did she begin the process to establish trust/credibility as an expert?

- ✓ Did she begin the process to establish a working relationship?
- ✓ Did she make a comfortable segue to the prospective clients need?
- ✓ Was the conversation pressure free?

I think you'll agree that she did meet all these criteria and more.

When you present this a couple of times you find that it feels increasingly natural and effective.

Now obviously these are my words using my speech patterns and personality type. Yours would be different. That's the reason you need to create and practice your own whispers. The story should come out of your mouth as relaxed and easy as if you're talking to a friend yet confident enough to inspire trust that you know what you're talking about.

CHAPTER 15

Networking Mindsets

Street Smart Rule #1: Actively work to create an island of safety and creativity for yourself in a networked village of your cohorts (Please, don't be that guy who waits till he's drowning then expects his network to throw him a life preserver)

— *Street-Smart Resources*

O ne of our culture's most enduring myths, especially to those of us who grew up in the West, are that a large measure of our success is how "self reliant" we are. After all, we're told, that's how the pioneers were.

Problem is—it's a myth—and a bad one to base your behavior on.

My grandparents homesteaded a place at the foot of the Beartooth Mountains near Red Lodge, Montana. They started with a virtual prairie wilderness and built a successful ranch. That first winter they lived in a tent along Volney Creek. And if you experienced a Montana winter or two you know how brutal that was. Along the way they raised five successful children.

The myth would have us believe they carved out a home by themselves with their own bare hands working from dawn to dusk.

And they did, of course, work hard and I can tell you back breaking work it was, but they also depended on a "network" of family and neighbors who helped them when they needed help and who they in turn helped.

Somebody got sick and they were there to lend a hand to help with the plowin'.

They all called it being neighborly. Ever hear of a "barn raisin'?

Of course, we're all sophisticated today, so we call it networking, but I'm thinking that we would be better off thinking of as it being neighborly. Networking sounds a little too self serving, and selfish networking is self destructive.

Good networking succeeds because it's honestly and unselfishly trying to lend a hand, or offer a bit of advice. Good politicians know that. They have to quickly build a web of favors in order to pass their agenda. So should you.

> "When was the last time you helped someone with the plowin'...."

So the first rule of good self-marketing is to master networking.

Consequential Strangers

I recently came across a book by Melinda Blau titled, "Consequential Strangers-Turning Everyday Encounters into Life Changing Moments". I love the title. If you're networking, you're looking for that "Consequential Stranger" to enter your life.

The more you network the better the odds. So make a pledge to get out of your comfort zone and meet folks, because opportunity is serendipitous. Look back on your own life. How many chance meetings led to massive changes in your life, a marriage, a career? Networking is non-linear— little things often lead to big effects.

So we take action. We walk right up and chat with that perfect stranger we meet at a cocktail party. And because we're armed with our whispers, we're confident.

Now, I'd be willing to bet good money that quite a few of you folks have a little voice in the back of your mind that's saying:

Oh I agree with you, all that stuff makes some sense, but I could never pull that off. I really hate that selling/pitching stuff. I'm shy with strangers and I get self conscious. Surely, you're not talking to me, I'm an introvert and everyone knows that it's the lucky extroverts that can pull that off.

People box themselves into comfort zones by telling themselves that they have no choice. I'm an introvert, they say, and everybody knows introverts don't do that whole self marketing thing well.

Introducing You—The Ambivert

First of all let's bust one of the common myths about behavior—the one says that "everybody knows" that there are only two basic personality types in the world-- the Introvert and the Extrovert. And it's the Extrovert and his corresponding Type-A behavior who is best equipped to sell things.

The rest of us, the shy retiring types, the studious types, the shy, uncomfortable in groups types, might just as well stay home—crouched in our dark little rooms— and leave the selling to the "natural" sales people. (Incidentally, that's another myth, there is no gene in the human DNA for selling, sales is a learned skill)

The reality is that personality types fall all along the common bell curve. Smack dab in the middle of that curve where most of us live, there is another type that social scientists call The Ambivert. Chances are good that that's the category you fall into. We are much more common than the folks in either extreme.

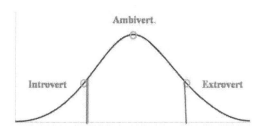

Personality/Behaviour Types

Ambivert.

Introvert   Extrovert

We ambiverts fall between the two extremes. We're not extremely introverted—we can actually leave our homes and venture out to work and we're not extremely extroverted—we're energized when we have some alone time.

We can assert ourselves when we *need* to but we're not pushy.

Sometimes we allow our inherent personality traits to box us into comfort zones.

However, according to researcher Brian Little's "free trait theory," it's possible to adjust these traits in order to advance "core personal projects," or projects that give you meaning and direction. In other words, your behavior traits are more malleable than you think.

So if you're hesitant to self-market because you're naturally more reserved, embrace the free trait theory and take on the guest role of an pseudo-extrovert for an hour in service of what matters to you.

In other words, "you can fake it till you make it"—if you have something of value to present. Ambiverts do it all the time for projects they believe in, for goals that move them toward a vision they really believe, if they don't let their comfort zone limit them.

Just do it!

If you were hoping for an easy button here, there isn't one. Like Nike says-- you just gotta do it.

That's the reason you build your Three Whispers. When you enter a room armed with them, you're confident and the battle is all but won. Like most things if you prepare properly, you prevent poor performance.

So go for it. Forget you're working. Relax; it's not that big a deal. You've had millions of conversations. You've paid your dues, just be yourself and have a good time. It's not rocket science—(unless of course you work for Orbital Sciences Corp.)

Put a smile on your face, walk up to that guy standing in the corner, stick out your hand and introduce yourself.

Then ask 'em what they do.

Then listen.

Then when asked give your 'simple whisper". Then let things flow where they may.

CHAPTER 16

Concluding Thoughts

Reframing is the ability to see things, problems, situations or people in other ways, to look at them sideways or upside-down, to put them in another perspective or context; to think of them as opportunities not problems, as hiccups rather than disasters. Reframing is important because it unlocks problems.

— *Charles Handy, "The Age of Unreason"*

This quote is particularly apropos to the central message of book—the necessity to re-frame some of your old ways of thinking and patterns of behavior. My goal was to encourage you to take an upside-down look at your Work and some of your long held beliefs. If you could do that you will have a pretty good shot at moving beyond the limitations they impose.

During my "apprenticeship" years, the thought never occurred to me that my hard work didn't speak for itself. It wasn't until I hit the turbulent late seventies and eighties that I began to realize that there was a problem.

Those years were characterized by destructively high rates of inflation which lead to hundreds of mergers and leveraged buyouts of old line companies. Thousands of careers were disrupted— mine among them.

I began to realize that I needed to take responsibility for my career— pretty disheartening for a guy who always trusted to unspoken promise of "we'll take care of you if you show up and work hard."

The problem was that I had no idea how to do it effectively. I had been taught all my life about the virtues of modesty. I couldn't see myself as a carnival pitchman.

Then came the reframing I mentioned in the early part of the book. When you joined me on this journey, the message was that you needed to acquire the knack and habit of "subtle" self marketing. That it was your responsibility to find a way to toot your own horn because no one was going to toot it for you. That in order to flourish, instead of merely survive, you needed to learn some basic self-marketing methods well enough to be able to weave them seamlessly into the way you do your Work.

Next I suggested that the way you thought about selling was probably incomplete, that the reason you needed to master the skill sets to sell/market was that before you could go to work on a problem or need your Work could easily take care of— you needed to correct the information imbalance. In order to do this you need to have a way to establish some trust.

Further, you have a powerful marketing tool at your disposal—The Story.

After combining your story and the story of your customer's dilemma you can build a series of Whispers that would do the job perfectly without hint of brag or puffery.

Whispers that would shout the marketing message your Work deserved— "No brag-Mister-just fact."

More importantly, the building of your story will grant you insight into your Work's excellence and give you the gift of self-confidence, freeing you from the limiting tyranny of your self talk

---

Setting Sails

I'd like to share a story about a friend of mine named Sean who lives on a sailboat. He invites me to go out with him occasionally, especially when he needs someone to help with some maintenance task.

I'm not a good sailor. It took me a while to get up the nerve to go out on his boat with him, I was far too manly to admit it, but being on a boat out of swimming distance to shore scared the hell out of me. Worse yet, his boat is a sailboat and it feels a bit sketchy to be at the random mercies of the wind.

When I explained the reason I refused so many of his invitations to join him, he laughed at me.

"Jesus, Pete, we have an auxiliary engine and the fact is that it's not the wind that determines where we sail, it's the guy who trims the sails. Grow a set and come down on Saturday"

The phrase "the guy who trims the sails" has stuck in my mind ever since.

Many of us feel our lives are out of our control. Like Sean's sailboat, we are constantly pushed and pulled by the undercurrents of circumstance. In 2008 we all experienced another major economic storm, (they show up with depressing regularity). That particular howling wind blew many of us off course and even wrecked some of us. Millions of folks had their illusions of financial security ripped away.

My hope is that this book gives you access to tools that will enable you to trim your sails by yourself and then turn chance into opportunity--serendipity into success. I wrote it to offer you a street-smart way to take back control of your destiny by giving your Work the marketing it deserves.

I promise you that if you practice the things in this book, something strange will happen. Something that Stephen Cesi has called the "Multiplier Effect" will take place. Because you will be armed with your Whispers, you will be much more confident than you were before. You're likely to feel good presenting yourself and because you feel good about being good at it, the drive to excel at it will engage and you will begin to concentrate and tweak it to make it more a function of your personality.

Your self-marketing will become a virtuous circle.

That's good news for your future.

Thank you for reading this book.

Peter K Young

About the Author

My name is Pete Young.

I'm a street guy--plain spoken and mostly self educated. Like everyone who gets to a certain age. My life experience is varied. I've been a hard rock miner, a five and dime store manager, a successful salesman, a sales trainer, a trade show producer, a boilermaker, sales and marketing consultant and a soybean oil commodity risk manager.

I am a relentless, compulsive autodidact.

Formal schooling didn't work too much for me (read I was bone lazy) but the lash and slings of fortune are effective teachers. The effective life lessons come when experience (usually not gently) point out the need for a new way of thinking—the teachable moment.

I've gone through three major career/life changes. All of them proved to be traumatic. All of them were also blessings well disguised. In all of them I went from expert to neophyte and very slowly back to expert. All of them gave richness to my Work.

I was completely unprepared to deal with the first two changes, the last was smoother, but none of them proved to be the romantic renewal experience I'd read about. Conception proved to be a lot more fun than the process of birth.

I served three "apprenticeships" only one of which was formal.

The first taught me to manage a business.

The second taught me sales and marketing.

The third taught me craftsmanship and discipline.

I have an irreverent sense of humor and very little self-importance (that's been pretty well beaten out of me).

But I'm passionate about the things I write about.

Made in the USA
San Bernardino, CA
20 September 2017